NARROW GAUGE BRANCH LINES

VIVARAIS
NARROW GAUGE
featuring Mallets in the Massif

John Organ

Series editor
Vic Mitchell

MP Middleton Press

Published to commemorate the 30th anniversary of the reopening of the Tournon - Lamastre line as the Chemin de Fer du Vivarais in July 1969.

Published May 1999

ISBN 1 901706 31 1

© Middleton Press, 1999

Design Deborah Esher

Published by
> *Middleton Press*
> *Easebourne Lane*
> *Midhurst, West Sussex*
> *GU29 9AZ*

Tel: 01730 813169
Fax: 01730 812601

Printed & bound by RPM Reprographics Ltd,
> *Chichester, West Sussex*

CONTENTS

ABBREVIATIONS

CFD	Chemins de Fer Départementaux
CFR	Chemins de Fer Régioneaux
CFTM	Chemins de Fer Touristiques et de Montagne
CFV	Chemin de Fer du Vivarais
ETAT	Chemin de Fer de l'Etat (French State Railway)
FACS	Fédération des Amis des Chemins de Fer Secondaires
PLM	Paris Lyon Mediterranean
POC	Paris Orléans Corrèze
RhB	Rhätische Bahn
SACM	Société Alsacienne de Constructions Mécaniques
SLM	Schweizerische Lokomotive und Maschinenfabrik
SNCF	Société Nationale des Chemins de Fer Francais
VFV	Voies Ferrées du Velay

ACKNOWLEDGEMENTS

This book could not have been written without much valuable assistance from many people. I must particularly thank Jean Arrivetz, President of the CFTM, who during the period of preparation has provided a vast amount of information in answer to my many requests. To all the following who have provided assistance in so many ways I offer my grateful thanks:

Mon J.Arrivetz, Mon F.Collardeau, Mr D.Trevor Rowe, Mr J.B.Snell, Mr J.Wiseman, Mon J.L.Rochaix, Bureau Vaudois d'Addresses, Mr V.J.Bradley, Mr K.Taylorson, Mr P.Pacey, Mr J.Marsh, Mr J.A.Wood, Mrs M.E.Sharman, Mrs R.Stone, Mrs S.J.Cornish, Mrs H.Marshall, and Mr J.L.Higgs.

Finally a special word of thanks to my wife Brenda who has patiently tolerated my deep involvement with the project. By adopting the attitude "if you can't beat them, join them" Brenda is now almost as enthusiastic about the subject as I am !

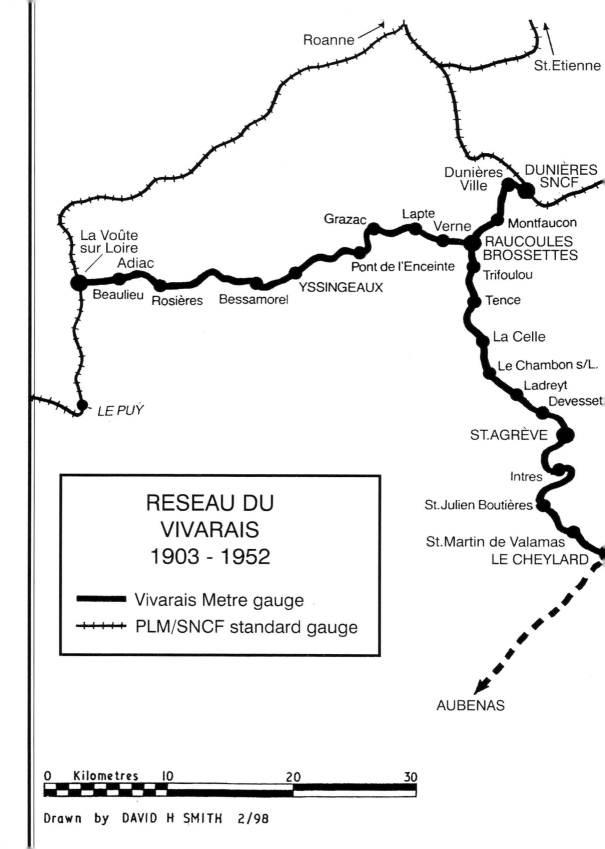

Roanne

St.Etienne

Dunières
Ville

DUNIÈRES
SNCF

Montfaucon

Grazac

Lapte

Verne

RAUCOULES
BROSSETTES

La Voûte
sur Loire

Adiac

Pont de l'Enceinte

Trifoulou

Beaulieu

Rosières

Bessamorel

YSSINGEAUX

Tence

La Celle

Le Chambon s/L.

Ladreyt

Devesset

LE PUŸ

ST.AGRÈVE

Intres

St.Julien Boutières

RESEAU DU
VIVARAIS
1903 - 1952

St.Martin de Valamas

LE CHEYLARD

——— Vivarais Metre gauge

+++++ PLM/SNCF standard gauge

AUBENAS

0   Kilometres   10   20   30

Drawn by DAVID H SMITH 2/98

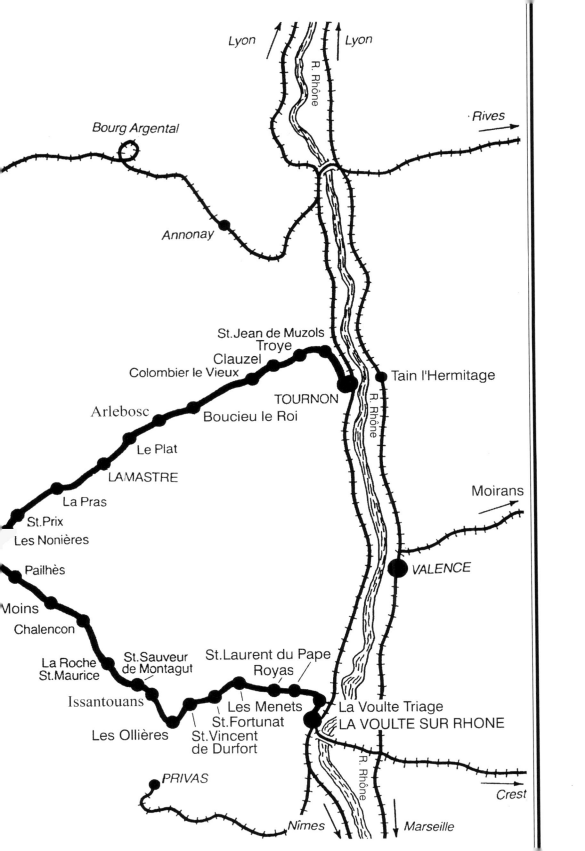

FOREWORD

After World War II, railways underwent a great change, brought about on the one hand by competition from road transport and on the other by the disappearance of steam traction in favour of electric or diesel traction. More than a century of industrial history was swept into the past, with its traditions, its hours of glory and its contributions to human progress.

In many countries, men started to take steps to safeguard some evidence of the world of coal and rail. The increase in tourism allowed the creation of a new activity, where technical history mixes with convivial rides through beautiful countryside.

In France, one was contented to preserve a few old locomotives and indeed to run them on short lines, (Meyzieu in 1961, St. Trojan in 1963, Pithiviers and Abreshviller in 1966). It was however in 1967 that a prick of conscience shook the French railway activists, principally after visits to the Talyllyn , Ffestiniog, Welshpool & Llanfair in Wales. We knew then that rapid action was necessary on the continent, to save the last beautiful lines with the last beautiful locomotives.

Precisely at that time, the superb Vivarais network succumbed to the recession. It had never taken on the principal task it had been given: to join the Rhône valley with the Loire valley. Little modernised, it did not touch the larger towns in the area. That is why at the end of 1968 a team of enthusiasts decided to exploit tourism with a branch of the 'Vivarais', between Tournon and Lamastre.

The authorities hardly gave it credibility, but left it to naive amateurs. When they saw it was a success, they were keen to sell the line. But those who had formed the company, did not forget the British example that had for 30 years guided their resolute daring. More than 2000 Anglophiles travel each year on the Vivarais. We try to stay true to the principles that the British have laid down. But it is amusing all the same to note that they call this a 'preserved railway', when we talk of a 'tourist railway', two different views of an achievement that we both recognise.

I hope that this book goes some way towards reasserting the 'entente cordiale' of the little trains of Europe and will remind tourists of the great times of the railwaymen of the past.

JEAN ARRIVETZ
PRESIDENT OF THE CFTM (VIVARAIS AND HAUT RHÔNE)
HON.VICE PRESIDENT FEDECRAIL
PATRON OF THE FFESTINIOG RAILWAY

Jean Arrivetz waves as he and the series editor are about to board the railway's first Santa Special, which ran on 20th December 1998. The inspection saloon was used as a grotto for *Pierre Nöel* and is described in caption 6.3. (V.Mitchell)

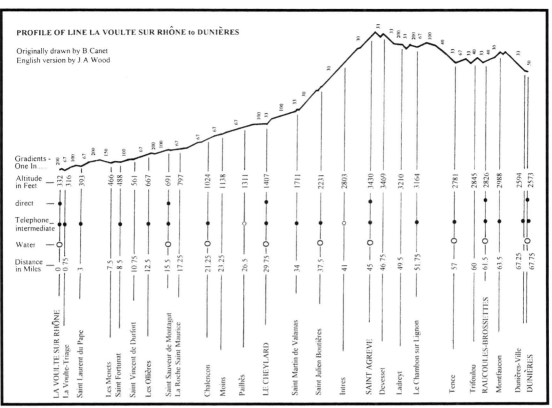

PROFILE OF LINE LA VOULTE SUR RHÔNE to DUNIÈRES

Originally drawn by B.Canet
English version by J.A Wood

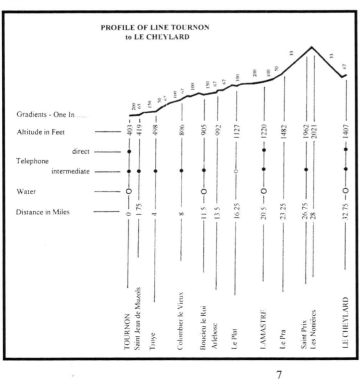

PROFILE OF LINE TOURNON
to LE CHEYLARD

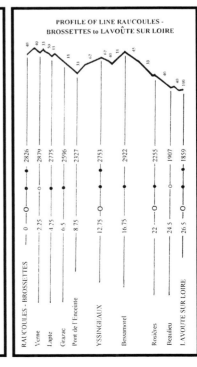

PROFILE OF LINE RAUCOULES -
BROSSETTES to LAVOÛTE SUR LOIRE

CHAPTER ONE

CHEMINS DE FER DÉPARTEMENTAUX
1890 – 1968

Communications and transport in rural France during the nineteenth century were, in common with the rest of Europe, sparse to say the least. By the 1860s the nucleus of a mainline railway network had been constructed and a scheme was formulated to add many minor lines to the system. Ultimately France boasted an incredible 17,000 miles of these minor railways, or *Secondaires*, many of them metre gauge or 60cm, crossing the less populous regions. These lines fell into two categories - *Intérêt Général* which were the more substantial concerns, and *Intérêt Local*. The former were answerable to the State and could be supported by it if they incurred losses, unlike the latter which benefited only the local communities and whose upkeep was the responsibility of the local *communes*. Many of the *Intérêt Général* lines were controlled by the major companies and ultimately became part of the State system, the SNCF. Notable among these were the *Réseau Breton* and the *PO Corrèze* which were originally controlled by the ETAT and Paris-Orléans respectively. These were large concerns compared to the *Intérêt Locals,* which were often no more than roadside tramways, many of them constructed by the Paul Decauville concern. Decauville built complete railway systems: permanent way, locomotives and rolling stock. Many of them were designed as portable railways, which could easily be moved to a different location if the need arose. They were put to excellent use among the sugar beet fields of northern France, having been adapted from former World War I military supply lines.

Apart from those lines under the wing of the major companies, the majority of the *Intérêt Général* undertakings were constructed and operated by the *Chemin de Fer Départementaux,* a company formed in 1881 to build and operate railways in areas in which the major companies were not interested. Ultimately the CFD controlled a total of thirteen railways throughout France in addition to the system in Corsica. The majority of these were metre gauge lines, although three were standard gauge, and were controlled by the CFD from its head office in Paris. By far the most famous and impressive of these railways was the *Réseau du Vivarais*, not only because of the terrain it covered but also in view of the impressive locomotives that were required to operate the line.

The railway was originally projected as early as 1862 with the intention of linking the main rivers each side of the Vivarais Mountains in the Massif Central. The two rivers were the Loire and the Rhône and, although the first section was opened in 1890, it was to be thirteen years later that the final link was completed in 1903. By this time the *Réseau du Vivarais* comprised a total of 126 miles, serving forty-one stations and halts. The highest point of the system was where it crossed the 3,000ft watershed of the Atlantic and Mediterranean, which required gradients as steep as 1 in 30 to reach it, including a continuous 10-mile stretch on the southern side at that grade. Sadly, this highly scenic and steeply-graded section between Le Cheylard and St Agrève is not part of either of the preserved sections, although the majority of the route is now a footpath. It includes two major viaducts and a succession of short tunnels hewn through rock outcrops.

Construction began in 1886 under the auspices of the CFD and the first section to be completed was a 14-mile line from La Voûte sur Loire to Yssingeaux, which was opened on 9th November 1890. This isolated stretch of line, which linked the western flank of the Velay Hills with the Loire Valley and the PLM line from St Etienne to Le Puy, was to remain the entire mileage of the infant *Réseau du Vivarais* until 1891, when two more lines were constructed far away in the east connecting with the PLM lines in the Rhône Valley. On 12th July the 20-mile line from Tournon to Lamastre, which provided the hitherto almost inaccessible Doux Valley with a link to the "outside world", began operations. Two months later, on 10th September, a 30-mile line from La Voulte sur Rhône to Le Cheylard was opened through the beautiful Eyrieux Valley. Although easier graded than its northern associates, this was a particularly difficult line to construct. It followed the river along the valley floor for much of the distance and required many tunnels and cuttings through the hard granite cliff sides. At both Tournon and La Voulte the metre gauge tracks joined the PLM route about a mile or so north of the respective towns, which required two sections of mixed gauge track to reach the terminal stations. In later years this route along the west bank of the Rhône became a freight-only line of the SNCF, passenger trains being confined to the electrified line on the east bank. This, of course, became something of a disadvantage for potential "through" passengers as it entailed a lengthy walk across the river to the mainline station - unless they were wealthy enough to afford a taxi!

Although it was at the head of a single branch line for over ten years, Le Cheylard was ultimately to become the headquarters of the Vivarais system, being at the hub of the envisaged network. Obviously, three isolated branch lines were only the first steps in the plan to link the Loire with the Rhône, but it was to be after the turn of the century that the ultimate aim was achieved. On 21st September 1902, Yssingeaux was connected with Dunières, providing a mainline connection with the PLM line from St Etienne to Annonay. A week later, on 27th September, a junction was created at Raucoules-Brossettes about six miles south of Dunières. From here the line over the watershed to St Agrève was opened on that date. On 7th December of that year the La Voulte-Le Cheylard line was extended to St Julien Boutières, leaving two heavily-graded sections to complete the system. The 29th May 1903 saw the highly scenic line from St Julien to St Agrève finally completed, whilst the final link in the system from Lamastre to Le Cheylard opened on 7th July of that year.

Most of the official openings of the various sections were fairly incident-free affairs, although accompanied by the usual French passion for an abundance of wine and good food. However, 10th September 1891 was notable for one official opening which didn't go exactly according to plan. The inaugural train from La Voulte sur Rhône to Le Cheylard, which was literally full to the point of overcrowding with local dignitaries, government officials and members of the press, proved too much for the small 2-6-0T locomotive and it had to be rescued by a sister locomotive. The result was an arrival at Le Cheylard three hours late, which did have one benefit for the assembled guests. With the roast roe deer about to fall off the bone, the usual never-ending speeches were postponed until the end of the meal about two hours later, by which time no one really paid much attention to them anyway!

For seventy-eight years the *Réseau du Vivarais* operated a regular service of passenger and freight traffic, the latter mainly timber - there was a huge demand for pitprops at the coalmines around St Etienne. In financial terms, the railway's golden years were just prior to World War I when, in 1913, it was at its peak. During that year it transported 664,000 passengers and 170,000 tons of goods, mainly timber, coal and farm produce. Many of the trains were mixed affairs, with cattle and sheep in their own vans whilst chickens and rabbits travelled with their owners in the passenger

1.1.   An SLM Mallet takes water alongside the workshop at Le Cheylard in 1905. (BVA Collection).

1.2. An early view of Le Cheylard shows the station prior to its enlargement in 1928.
(Coll. J.L. Rochaix /BVA).

1.3. SACM 0-4-4-OT Mallet No.63 was photographed shortly after delivery in 1891.
(Collection. K. Taylorson).

1.4. SLM Mallet No.403 shunts at Le Cheylard on 12th May 1963. (J. L. Rochaix /BVA).

1.5.   Timber awaits shipment at Le Cheylard in 1946. (Coll. Dr.Brenot /BVA).

coaches. The 1913 figures produced operating expenses expressed as a proportion of receipts as low as 0.75 - a figure which the CFD would look back on with envy in later years. With such a successful period behind it, thoughts were directed to extending the line even further into a hitherto untapped area. The plan was for a line over the mountains from Le Cheylard to Aubenas about thirty miles to the south. The route was surveyed, and in 1920 provisional plans for some powerful Mallet locomotives to work the line were prepared. However, with the steady increase in road transport in the years following World War I, the scheme never progressed further and it remains a tantalising "what might have been" piece of railway history.

The area covered by the Vivarais system extended over two *Départementaux*, the Ardèche (which roughly equates with the old Vivarais province) housing most of the line, whilst the northern section beyond the watershed was in the neighbouring Haute-Loire. This southern part of the Massif Central is an area of outstanding scenic beauty, with its rugged gorges, extensive vine terraces and high plateaux, and yet it is an area largely unknown to many people. Lying between the two main routes to the south, it was unjustifiably ignored by a large majority of tourists from the north, with the result that the *Réseau du Vivarais* relied largely upon local patronage for the majority of its traffic. During the 1920s the railway continued to prosper, with a record number of 680,000 passenger journeys in 1929. However, these figures did not equate to an increase in profit as wages and expenses had increased after World War I more than the railway revenue. In an attempt to compete with the ever-growing amount of road transport, a fleet of railcars was introduced during the 1930s which took over most of the passenger workings. Still the returns continued to show a negative balance, apart from a positive increase during World War II. During this period the *Vivarais,* which was in the heart of Resistance country, ran guns concealed in coal trucks for the Maquis. This activity did have its recompense when the yards at Le Cheylard were attacked in July 1944, resulting in three locomotives and other stock being damaged beyond repair. This was the period following the D-Day landings, when much of the German army in the south of France was re-deployed to the north, and basically "shot anything that moved" whilst on their way!

The wartime years were in many ways quite a profitable period. This was partly due to the fact that the inhabitants of this largely rural area had to rely on the railway for both commuting and freight, due to the lack of alternative forms of transport during the period of hostilities. With the onset of peace, although the *Réseau du Vivarais* remained a "lifeline" for many of the inhabitants of the area, it was also a period of change. Private cars, buses and the inevitable lorries slowly began to

1.6.   Billard A-150-D No.213 collects passengers in a timeless scene at St. Martin-de-Valamas in July 1962. (D. Trevor Rowe).

make their way back into circulation, gathering momentum as the decade drew to an end. In an attempt to compete with the ever-growing alternative forms of transport, various means of trying to increase the railway service were tried. A short-lived non-stop railcar service between La Voulte and Dunières was operated without a great deal of success in 1949, whilst the faster and more nimble railcars continued to handle the majority of the passenger traffic. Steam was largely used for freight workings, although a number of mixed passenger and freight trains continued to be operated, mainly in connection with market days.

During the late 1940s the financial returns continued to fall, so it was obvious that drastic action would have to be taken. The line from La Voûte sur Loire to Raucoules-Brossettes (which included the original La Voûte-Yssingeaux section) was found to be operating at a coefficient of 4.64, which equated to a mere 22p in revenue for every £1.00 spent in operation, obviously a situation that could not be allowed to continue. So the La Voûte line closed on 29th February 1952, leaving 101 miles, which continued to be operated for a further sixteen years. During this period the CFD, in an attempt to operate a more efficient and cost-effective service, drafted in additional railcars, which were transferred from the *Réseau Charentes* in western France, when that line closed. In addition, a small fleet of diesel locomotives supplemented the steam workings on freight trains.

By the late 1960s the steam locomotives had virtually all been retired. Those not already scrapped were stored awaiting their fate, but fortunately two Mallets were retained in working order. Officially they were retained for emergency use, such as during the winter months when they were fitted with snowploughs in order to clear a path for the light-footed railcars during periods of extreme weather. As in most countries, the enthusiasm for steam died hard and the presence of these two surviving locomotives on the *Vivarais* soon became noted. In a brave public relations exercise, the CFD promoted numerous "last steam excursions" over the line, hauled by one of the two survivors. In fact, on one notable occasion in 1968, such was the demand for seats that both locomotives and every available coach was used for what was virtually the swansong of the *Réseau du Vivarais*. Despite vehement opposition, mainly from enthusiasts, it was obvious that the CFD could not continue to incur the losses from everyday operation. Eventually the fateful day arrived and on 31st October 1968, the last railcars, draped in black cloth, made their way through the valleys for the last time.

1.7. SACM 0-6-6-OT Mallet No. 414 waits with a Dunières bound passenger train at Le Chambon-sur-Lignon in 1946. (Coll. Dr. Brenot /BVA).

1.8. Fives-Lille 2-6-OT No. 61 hauls a load or empty timber wagons at St. Julien-Boutières on 21ʳᵗ September 1954. (F. Collardeau /BVA).

CHAPTER TWO

ROUTES OF THE RÉSEAU DU VIVARAIS

The topography of the Vivarais system was most impressive and very varied. A typical journey over the line in the 1950s is described to illustrate that statement. (More recent comment is in italic). The wide black line on the track diagrams indicates standard gauge.

Dunières to Tence

The standard gauge SNCF line terminates here, although originally it used to continue over the hills and through a spiral tunnel to Annonay and down into the Rhône Valley. Across the yards and sidings, *most of which are now lost under a new road scheme*, is a small station comprising a booking office, single road engine shed, coal stage, turntable and stone-built water tower alongside the metre gauge track. This is the northern terminal station of the Vivarais.

Joining the waiting railcar, the driver sounds the twin-tone horns before leaving Dunières station. Almost immediately the railcar plunges into a short tunnel under the lower part of this hillside town, emerging at another station named Dunières Ville, which, as the name implies, is nearer the town centre than the junction station. Ville station consists simply of a single platform, with a chalet-type building comprising a station house and booking office, with a passing loop alongside. Leaving Dunières Ville, the line crosses a small level crossing and immediately begins a 4-mile climb on a 1 in 33 gradient. This incline through the wooded slopes of the Velay Hills follows the D61 road as it winds its way up the steep grade, with some fine vantage points where it emerges from the trees. At the top of the climb the railcar rolls into the station at Montfaucon, another typical French wayside station with a chalet-type building. To the north of the station is a long siding, probably full of goods trucks. After leaving Montfaucon the line leaves the road and begins an undulating and very twisty route across the Velay Hills towards Tence. Two miles from Montfaucon is the junction at Raucoules-Brossettes, where the line down to La Voûte sur Loire diverged to the right prior to its closure in 1952. The layout at Raucoules-Brossettes comprises another chalet-type building alongside the road to Brossettes village, a small single road engine shed, stone water tower and extensive sidings. At the far end of these the La Voûte line left the main line. Opposite the station building are two "garage"-type fuel pumps which are used by the railcars and other diesel-powered locomotives for topping up their tanks.

The 25-mile route to La Voûte sur Loire begins as another undulating route across the hills to Yssingeaux, with two major civil engineering features at its lowest points. These are the steel viaduct at Pont de l'Enceinte and the impressive parallel masonry viaducts at Chapelette where the line runs alongside the D105 as they both cross the Lignon Gorge. After Yssingeaux the original section of the *Réseau du Vivarais* begins with a descent at 1 in 66 followed by a climb at 1 in 33 to a summit at Bessamorel. From the summit there follows a 10-mile descent at an average gradient of 1 in 35 to La Voûte, where the line crosses the River Loire over a 3-span steel viaduct. This part of the *Vivarais* closed in 1952 and sadly there is little left now. It must have been a spectacular line to traverse, with some splendid scenery along the undulating route.

Raucoules-Brossettes, as its name implies, serves two villages, neither of which is within easy walking distance of the station. In fact, Raucoules is nearer to Montfaucon than the station bearing its name! Continuing the journey south from Raucoules-Brossettes, the route meanders across the plateau with hardly a length of straight track along the four and a half miles to the next station at the important market town of Tence. Here there is quite a large layout, with the station building alongside a level crossing at the southern end of the town. These chalet-type buildings were to be found all over France and were built to a basically standard design by the CFD. They comprised a simple booking office and waiting room downstairs, with living accommodation on the first floor and basic toilet facilities outside! Tence has quite a long yard with a number of sidings, at the far end of which is a turntable, single road engine shed and stone water tower. These three items of infrastructure are also typical CFD products and, like the station buildings, could be seen throughout France. The water towers are circular stone buildings with round steel water tanks on top. The water emerges from halfway up the stone base, and at a water column near the level crossing at the other end of the station.

The Vivarais section in the July 1913 edition of Bradshaw's timetable.

DUNIERES

To Le Cheylard

2.1.   SLM Mallet No.403 climbs out of Dunières with an empty freight working on 20th April 1963. (F. Collardeau)

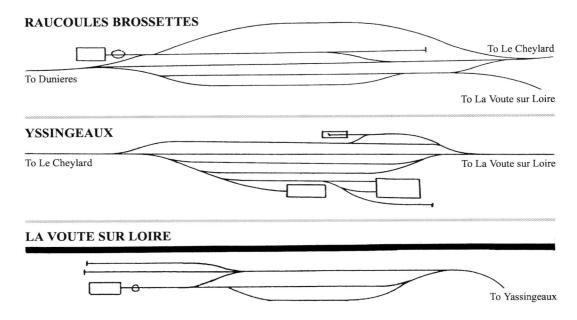

RAUCOULES BROSSETTES

To Le Cheylard

To Dunieres

To La Voute sur Loire

YSSINGEAUX

To Le Cheylard

To La Voute sur Loire

LA VOUTE SUR LOIRE

To Yassingeaux

2.2. One of the SLM Mallets hauls a mixed train across the viaduct at Chapalette towards Dunières on 8th September 1949. (F. Collardeau /BVA).

2.3. A Billard A-15O-D-2 Articulated Railcar rounds a curve between Yssingeaux and Bessamorel en route to La Voûte-sur-Loire on 16th August 1951. This view shows the trailing end car before the radiator was removed and the aperture blanked off. (F. Collardeau /BVA).

2.4. A timber train was recorded between Tence and Raucoules-Brossettes hauled by SLM Mallet No.407 fitted with a snow plough on 13th February 1954. (F. Collardeau /BVA).

TENCE

To Le Cheylard

To Dunieres

Tence to St Agrève

Leaving Tence, the line begins to climb at an average of 1 in 40 through the delightful upper reaches of the Lignon Gorge, following the D103 road to the next station at Le Chambon-sur-Lignon. This small town has become, in recent years, a developing winter sports centre, for we are now approaching the highest part of the route. Leaving Le Chambon there is a short descent at 1 in 33 before the climb into the Auvergnat Hills and the summit at the watershed of the Atlantic and Mediterranean at an altitude of over 3,500 feet. Here the landscape is barren and snowfences protect the line, for winters in this area can be quite severe. Whilst crossing the watershed, the line also passes from the Haute-Loire region into the Ardèche. A short distance further along the line and twelve miles after leaving Tence it drops down into the station at St Agrève, situated at the northern end of this small town which, like Le Chambon, is developing into a winter sports centre. St Agrève also has extensive sidings, where large stockpiles of timber were stored alongside awaiting loading on to wagons for shipment on to Dunières and the SNCF. Unlike Tence and Dunières, the engine shed is a two-road building alongside the station building on the other side of the running line. The turntable and water tower are a short distance away near the sidings.

ST AGREVE

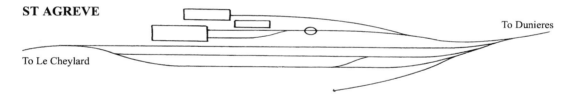

To Dunieres

To Le Cheylard

2.5.   Billard A-150-D hauling a type RM luggage van arrives at St. Agrève on 11th May 1963. Note the hand operated level crossing barrier pole. (J.L. Rochaix /BVA).

Note: The track from Dunières to St Agrève is still in place, and a limited summer diesel-hauled service has operated twice weekly between Dunières and Tence since 1994. The track between Tence and St Agrève is largely hidden beneath the undergrowth, having not been used for over ten years; it will require much attention before trains can run over it again. However, the track is still there, unlike the next section of the route, which is now a footpath through what was the most dramatic and scenic part of the Vivarais system.

St Agrève to Le Cheylard

We now return to our journey in the 1950s. Departing from St Agrève the railcar passes between the station and engine shed and, with a fanfare from its twin-tone horns, almost immediately traverses a level crossing. There then begins a 10-mile twisting descent at 1 in 30 as the line runs around a "horseshoe" at the end of the Eyrieux valley. Two major viaducts, the 7-arch Bon Pas and 5-arch Intres, are crossed, plus a series of short tunnels, during the journey. The driver, disregarding the fact that super-elevation of the track varied considerably between excessive and virtually non-existent, swings the railcar through the multitude of curves at around 40 mph, and the ride is exciting, to say the least! The scenery through the wide valley is most impressive, from high on a ledge above the infant Eyrieux, with the ruined Château de Rochebonne on top of a rocky pinnacle dominating the scene on the approach to St Julien Boutières. It was for this section of the line that the large Mallets were primarily introduced. With such a length of severe gradients and excessive curvature, powerful locomotives were required but without the drawback of a long fixed wheelbase. The flexible Mallets are ideal for the purpose and hauling heavy timber-laden freight trains up the gradients is well within their capabilities. Apart from the deviation to La Voûte sur Loire, our journey from Dunières so far has been over the later section of the system, which opened in 1903. The line from Le Cheylard to Dunières, with its arduous gradients, was constructed with heavier rail on two sections - 46lb in 36ft lengths as opposed to 41lb in 24ft lengths on the older and easier-graded sections.

2.6.   FACS special hauled by No.403 crosses the viaduct at Intres during the steep ascent from Le Cheylard to St. Agrève on 24th July 1966. Note the Articulated Billard Railcar attached to the rear of the train. (J. L. Rochaix /BVA).

After passing the wayside station of St Julien Boutières, where a number of retired locomotives were stored, the 1 in 30 descent continues for a further three and a half miles to the next station at St Martin de Valamas. Here the descent eases considerably to 1 in 100 for the final four and a half miles to Le Cheylard. This descent continues to follow the now growing Eyrieux, the track still on a ledge above the river and running through more tunnels hewn through rock outcrops. The whole scene is somewhat reminiscent of the Aberglaslyn Pass in North Wales but on a much larger and grander scale! The line crosses the river for the last time across a steel girder bridge at the bottom of the gorge and finally enters the outskirts of Le Cheylard. Since leaving St Agrève at over 3,000ft, it has now descended to 1,420ft. Just to the south of St Agrève it crosses the 45th parallel, which denotes the division between the north and the south of France. Already the scenery has begun to adopt a Mediterranean image, with vine terraces on the hillsides in contrast to the bleak and barren landscape of the Auvergnat Plateau.

2.7.   Billard A-150-D-2 Articulated Railcar stands at St. Julien-Boutières on 6th July 1958. Note the blanked off radiator aperture on the trailing end car. (M. Dehanne/BVA).

LE CHEYLARD

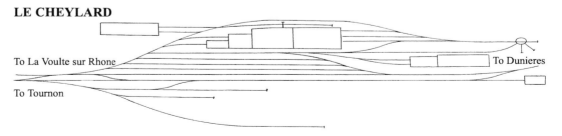

To La Voulte sur Rhone

To Dunieres

To Tournon

2.8. A freight train hauled by SACM Mallet No.414 pauses at St.Martin-de-Valamas en route to Le Cheylard on 24th August 1957. (F. Collardeau/BVA-CFTM).

2.9. SLM Mallet No.404,CFD Diesel Tractor Y and Fives-Lille 2-6-0T No.61 are on shed at Le Cheylard on 11th July 1954. (F. Collardeau/BVA)

2.10.   SLM Mallet No.401 is seen during a heavy overhaul in the workshop at Le Cheylard in September 1958. (J.B. Snell).

Le Cheylard is approached on a sweeping curve through the northern outskirts of this busy small industrial town before our railcar passes under a road bridge and arrives at the station complex. Situated on a shelf about a quarter of a mile in length alongside the river at the south of the town, Le Cheylard has been described as the "Crewe of the Vivarais". Here are the workshops and administrative offices of the system, in addition to the station and locomotive sheds. The station building, approached from the road by a short ramp, is a larger version of the chalet-type design elsewhere on the line. As well as the usual booking office and waiting rooms, there are additional offices plus the usual living accommodation upstairs. Adjacent to the station building is a large goods shed astride transhipment sidings, with road access along its rear wall. Opposite the station buildings on the far side of the multitude of tracks and crossovers is a three-road engine shed, immediately behind which is a fully equipped workshop which has the capabilities to tackle anything from routine maintenance to complete heavy overhauls.

This large building fell into a very poor state of repair following the closure of the Vivarais *in 1968 and it looked as if it was destined to be demolished. However, it has recently been restored to its former glory and adapted for use by the local bus company -* sic transit gloria*!!!*

In front of the engine shed is the carriage and wagon workshop which was also used for the maintenance of the railcars, whilst in the corner of the site alongside the river and road bridge is the usual water tower, coal stage and turntable. Alongside the coal stage are the workshop offices and stores, in addition to the usual facilities for the use of the workshop staff.

Le Cheylard is the hub of the system, situated at an important junction where the line from Dunières divides. To the south the line to La Voulte sur Rhône continues to follow the Eyrieux, whilst to the east the Tournon line climbs over another summit before descending the valley of the River Doux. To accentuate the importance of Le Cheylard, a poster map is painted on the station approach wall. This set Le Cheylard as a hub of communications throughout France, with lines reaching out to far off places such as Marseille, St Etienne, Lyon, Paris and beyond.

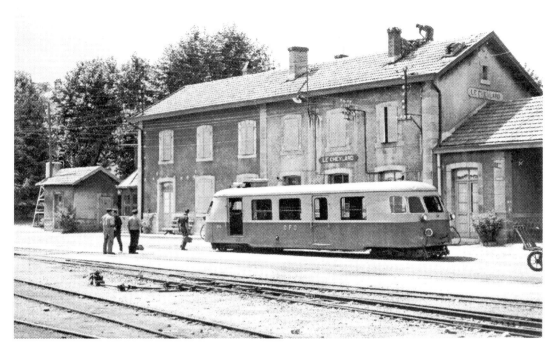

2.11.   Billard A-80-D Railcar No.316 waits in front of the enlarged station building at Le Cheylard on 24th July 1966. (J. L. Rochaix/BVA).

Le Cheylard to La Voulte sur Rhône

We now board again the railcar in the 1950s. The two lines leave Le Cheylard in an easterly direction, running parallel for a short distance before the La Voulte line veers off to the right, following the river. The highly scenic 30-mile journey to La Voulte runs alongside the Eyrieux on a fairly gentle gradient of 1 in 67 at its steepest. Despite the lack of vertiginous hillside stretches, it was a line full of heavy civil engineering features with many tunnels blasted through rock outcrops and buttressed viaducts alongside the cliff faces. During the course of our journey down the valley we pass through Pailhès, Chalencon and Les Ollières, where we cross the river over the viaduct at de Moulinas. At St. Fortunat the viaduct de La Pimpie takes the line across the river again before it continues to wind its way between the vineyards, passing Les Menets and St Laurent du Pape prior to joining the SNCF at La Voulte Triage. The final mile is along a mixed gauge track shared with the Lyon-Nîmes line along the west bank of the Rhône, passing through a short tunnel under the town.

The mixed gauge section, incorporating a third rail between the standard gauge tracks, was originally interlaced with both north and southbound lines of the SNCF (originally the PLM). The connections at each end of the section were made via a complex arrangement of switchless points.

In later years the layout was simplified in conjunction with modernised signalling prior to the electrification of the SNCF route. This simplified layout resulted in the metre gauge track being interlaced with only the northbound SNCF track. Modern signalling and track circuiting meant that two-way operation was possible along the mixed gauge section.

La Voulte sur Rhône is an important junction. Not only is it the southern terminus of the Vivarais system but in addition there is a triangular junction on the SNCF. From this junction a line crosses the Rhône to connect with the main line from Lyon to Marseille. The southern arm of the

2.12. An A-150-D-2 Articulated Billard was recorded shortly after leaving Le Cheylard, bound for La Voulte-sur-Rhône in September 1958. Note the bathers in the river enjoying the hot weather. (J. B. Snell).

2.13. 22nd September 1968 saw the final steam hauled passenger train. No.403 is seen here working from La Voulte-sur-Rhône shortly before arriving at Le Cheylard. (J. Wiseman).

2.14.   This is a photograph stop at the Viaduct de la Pimpie at St.Fortunat for one of the final special trains on 22nd September 1968. The formation comprises of two A-150-D-2 Articulated Billards with two R-210 trailer cars in the centre. (J. Wiseman).

2.15.   A FACS special arrives at La Voulte-Triage on 12ᵗʰ May 1963. (J. L. Rochaix/BVA).

LA VOULTE TRIAGE

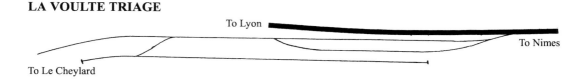

junction at La Voulte actually crosses the Nîmes line via a level crossing before swinging round to join the main line south of the station.

The CFD station at La Voulte is a very compact site alongside the SNCF immediately to the north of the standard gauge level crossing. The station buildings serves both the *Vivarais* and the SNCF and are situated on the far side of the mainline tracks. In the southern corner of the CFD part of the complex is a two-road engine shed and the usual water tower, turntable and coal stage. Considering the importance of the PLM/SNCF junction at La Voulte, the CFD part of the complex is a fairly modest affair compared with the combined station twenty miles to the north at Tournon.

The Lyon-Nimes route is now a very busy freight-only line, unlike the Marseille line which handles mainly passenger traffic. With two such diverse routes each side of the Rhône, this connecting line between La Voulte and Livron is very important, continuing eastwards through Crest and towards the Alps at Gap and Briancon.

2.16.   Mallet No.403 passes over the level crossing at La Voulte-Triage with a mixed train bound for Le Cheylard on 8th September 1965. (F. Collardeau).

2.17.   Billard A-150-D-2 and A-80-D Railcars at La Voulte-sur-Rhône on 22nd September 1968. (J. Wiseman).

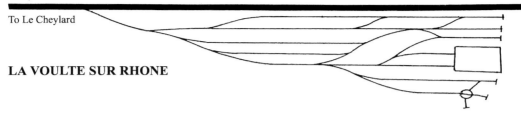

To Le Cheylard

LA VOULTE SUR RHONE

Le Cheylard to Tournon

Returning to Le Cheylard we rejoin our railcar for the final part of the journey over the *Vivarais* system. Leaving the station we pass through the extensive yards with the locomotive shed and workshops on the right. The Tournon line runs parallel with the La Voulte line until the latter curves away to the right and follows the River Eyrieux. After the two lines diverge, the railcar begins to climb a gradient of 1 in 33 for four and a half miles, mostly following the D578 road to the summit at Les Nonières. The major engineering feature of this part of the line is the 6-arch viaduct at St Cierge, where the line crosses the road for the first time. The summit at Les Nonières is unusual in that it is the only one on the Vivarais system that is in a tunnel. This passes under the village.

After leaving the 800-yard tunnel the line begins to descend at the same 1 in 33 gradient as the ascent from Le Cheylard. After the route crosses the road again at the 5-arch viaduct at St Prix, the

2.18.   A-150-D-2 Railcar crosses the viaduct at St. Cierge with a Tournon to Le Cheylard service on 12ᵗʰ May 1963. (J. L. Rochaix/BVA).

2.19.   SLM Mallet No.406 is seen with a Lamastre bound freight train on the viaduct at St. Prix on 21st September 1954. (F. Collardeau/BVA-CFTM).

scenery begins to resemble that between St Agrève and Le Cheylard, albeit on not such a grand scale. The 6-mile descent to Lamastre continues via La Pras, where the gradient eases to 1 in 50. As Lamastre is approached we cross a steel viaduct over the River Sumène before the line becomes a roadside railway for about half a mile, after which we pass a gated level crossing near the confluence of the Rivers Doux and Sumène, shortly before coming to a halt at the station.

Lamastre station is in a beautiful setting near the centre of this pleasant town, which over the years has gained a reputation as a gastronomic centre. Here there is the usual CFD structures of station building, single-road engine shed, turntable, coal stage, water tower and goods shed, all neatly grouped together at one end of the extensive sidings. These, as with many others on the system, would have seen large stockpiles of timber ready for loading on to wagons parked alongside. The station building is one of the larger variations of the standard CFD design, which would suggest that this was a station of some importance.

Leaving Lamastre, our railcar journey continues initially along a roadside section for about half a mile through a tree-lined avenue. At the outer limits of the town the line leaves the D534 and begins to descend the Doux Valley on a gentle gradient of 1 in 100 at its maximum. We are now heading north-east and shortly after leaving Lamastre we pass a large sign denoting that we have once again crossed the 45th parallel - midway between the Equator and the North Pole. Entering the first part of the Doux Gorge the line is again on a ledge above the river opposite the pretty village of Empurany. At the level crossing at Le Plat, there is a short climb past the halt of the same name before descending again to cross the river twice at the viaducts at Le Garnier and Le Banchet. Over-

LAMASTRE

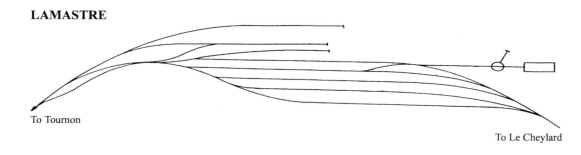

To Tournon

To Le Cheylard

2.20. SLM Mallet No.403 waits during its lunchtime rest at Lamastre on 3ʳᵈ September 1996. It is on the turntable siding. (Mrs B. Organ).

looking the latter 6-arch structure is a stone perched precariously on top of a rock outcrop. This is known as *The Turning Stone* and local legend suggests that it turns every hundred years. However, no one seems to know when it last happened!

After crossing the Doux at Le Banchet, we leave the river and run through an area of meadows and agricultural land, passing the halt at Tincey before entering the next station at Boucieu Le Roi, nine miles from Lamastre. The scene here is dominated by a large monastery on top of the hill near the village, which became a school for delinquent children. A short distance away, near Tincey, is a prominent round grass-covered hill with three crosses on its summit. This re-creation of Calvary is reached by a footpath from Boucieu Le Roi along which there are a number of small chapels, one of which is seen alongside the line at the level crossing, about half a mile south of the station.

Facilities at Boucieu Le Roi are pretty basic, a typical CFD station building, water tower serving two water columns, a passing loop and a small siding. Immediately to the north of the station

2.21. Billards bask in the sun at Lamastre in September 1992. From left to right is No.314, one of the R-210 trailer cars and   No.213. (J. F. Organ).

2.22. SACM Mallet No.413 drifts into Colombier le Vieux with an afternoon train in August 1994. (J. F. Organ).

2.23.   Billard No.213 waits at Colombier le Vieux during the lunch break, while on an afternoon working from Lamastre to Tournon in September 1992. (J. F. Organ).

we go over another level crossing before rejoining the course of the river, although it is hardly visible through the trees which line this part of the route. After a further three and a half miles we arrive at a small station with a large name. Colombier Le Vieux-St Barthélemy Le Plain serves two villages of the same names, both of which are some distance away above each side of the valley. The station, in its beautiful setting, consists of nothing more than a CFD building and a bar. *It achieved a claim to fame in 1971 when the BBC used it as the location for the railway sequences in their production of Clochemerle.*

Almost immediately after leaving this tranquil setting we re-emerge on a ledge above the river for the journey down the lower part of the Doux Gorge. The next five miles are most impressive, although the gradients are less severe than on the highly scenic sections further north, 1 in 45 being the steepest gradient on this section. To the left on the other side of the gorge can be seen a canal built by German prisoners of war during World War I as part of a hydro-electric scheme. The canal eventually crosses the river and railway in an aqueduct near a small halt named Clauzel. During World War II, the French Resistance used this small isolated station to store weapons and ammunition which had been delivered by train hidden under coal and other merchandise. Beyond Clauzel the river makes a large horseshoe curved detour which the railway bypasses through a short curved tunnel. Far below the northern portal of this tunnel, at Mordane, is the hydro-electric power station, access to which is by a very steep footpath. Continuing down the gorge along the hillside ledge and buttressed viaducts, we eventually cross the river again over the curved viaduct at Troye, which incorporates a footpath alongside the track. As the line continues to follow the Doux, which is now on our right, we see a pumping station for the town of Tournon shortly after the point where the River

2.24. An elevated view of the fine viaduct at Troye shows Pinguely 0-6-0T No. 31 hauling a Lamastre-Tournon train on 14th July 1979. (F. Collardeau/CFTM).

2.25. The loop at St. Jean de Muzols was little used when photographed in 1998. This is the view towards Tournon. (V.Mitchell)

2.26. The CFV diverges from the northbound freight line at this point, which is devoid of moving parts. The bridge over the Doux and part of Tournon are in the background. (V.Mitchell)

To Lyon   To Nimes

To Le Cheylard

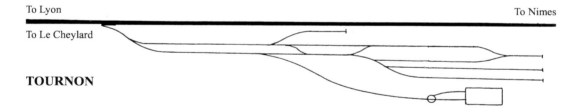

TOURNON

Duzon joins the Doux. The central pillar of the dam is constructed from stones that once formed part of a Roman road, this area at one time being the northern border of the Roman Empire before their advances further north. As we round the next curve we see the imposing arch of the bridge at Douce Plage. This fifteenth-century bridge over the Doux was the largest single-arch bridge in the world at the time of its construction. It took over one hundred years to build, the incomplete works being continually washed away by floods. Passing under the abutments of this large structure, the scenery immediately changes as we follow the D238 past the vineyards of St Joseph.

At St Jean de Muzols our railcar comes to a halt whilst the driver awaits clearance to join the dual-gauge section along the SNCF for the final mile and a half to Tournon.

Having received clearance by telephone, the railcar climbs up a short incline on to the SNCF Lyon-Nîmes line. As at La Voulte, the connections at each end of the dual-gauge section were originally via complex arrangements of switchless points connected to both tracks of the standard gauge. During the later years of the CFD operation this was simplified in conjunction with modernised signalling to connect with the northbound SNCF track only. Almost immediately after joining the

2.27. The track layout at Tournon is seen in 1951 when both lines of the SNCF were dual gauge. Bidirectional running on the metre gauge line on the right began in the 1950s and the other third rail was lifted later. The level crossing was also removed. (Photo F. Collardeau/CFTM)

standard gauge, we cross the Doux for the last time over a large lattice girder bridge before entering the first of two tunnels under the town of Tournon. After emerging from the second, and shorter, of these tunnels, the metre gauge track leaves the SNCF via another set of switchless points as our railcar swings to the right before coming to a halt in Tournon station.

The layout at Tournon consists of a small booking office and waiting room alongside the two running lines, the main station buildings being across the SNCF tracks on the far platform. Beyond the two stations are extensive sidings of both gauges, whilst to the right of the metre gauge yard is a two-road engine shed with a workshop behind it. In front of the engine shed, which is quite large, being capable of housing four locomotives, is the turntable, coal stage and water tower.

Unlike La Voulte, there is no line linking the freight-only Nîmes route with the Marseille line on the east bank of the Rhône. Therefore, travellers wishing to continue their journey by rail are faced with either a long walk or taking a taxi across one of the suspension bridges to the twin town of Tain l'Hermitage.

Tournon's origins go back to Roman times, but its more recent history is notable for being the home of the nineteenth-century engineer, Marc Seguin. In addition to inventing the water-tube boiler in 1852, he also designed a suspension bridge that spanned the Rhône at this point. This bridge was sadly demolished shortly after World War II, but a later structure survives as a footbridge between the two towns. Road traffic uses a modern concrete bridge a short distance downstream.

Having arrived at Tournon, we have completed our journey over the *Réseau du Vivarais*. This has taken us from the Haute-Loire to the Ardèche by one of the finest narrow gauge routes in Europe. From the wild barren landscape of the Velay and Auvergnat Hills to the high narrow ledges of the Eyrieux and Doux Gorges, the journey has been one of many contrasts and constant interest.

2.28.   Mallet No. 404 arrives at Tournon with a timber train In August 1960. In the background a SNCF 141R is seen passing through the standard gauge station. Regular passenger service on the main line ceased in 1972.   (F. Collardeau/CFTM).

2.29.   Assorted motive power was recorded at Tournon in August 1994.From left to right is Billard A-l50-D No. 213, Pinguely No. 31, Corpet No. 24 and Mallets 404 and 414.   (J. F. Organ).

CHAPTER THREE

OPERATING THE RÉSEAU DU VIVARAIS

The *Vivarais* was a very substantially constructed railway. The track, albeit of fairly light section rail on the older parts of the route, was well laid and maintained to a high standard. The earthworks included numerous stone-built embankments incorporating buttressed viaducts where the line ran on a ledge high above the various gorges. In addition there were many impressive viaducts where it crossed the valleys and an equally large number of tunnels where the rock became too impenetrable to avoid. As previously mentioned, station buildings were all of a standard design, well built in varying sizes depending upon the importance of the station. With the exception of the crossing at Lamastre, all the level crossings were ungated, relying on speed restrictions and much whistling for safety! In more recent years all the major crossings on the preserved CFV have been equipped with electrically operated half barriers and flashing lights.

Despite all this excellent infrastructure, one thing that was conspicuous by its absence was signalling of the conventional type. Apart from chequer-board signals at Tournon and La Voulte, where the metre gauge tracks merged with the standard gauge, the whole system was controlled by telephone. Should a train be halted for any reason in mid-section, it was protected by detonators and sight. This system still prevails today on the preserved lines, and its efficiency was demonstrated to the author in 1991. On this occasion three trains were following each other from Tournon to Lamastre - two steam-hauled and a railcar. As a result of a delayed departure due to a late-running SNCF freight train, the Mallet hauling the first train ran short of water before reaching Boucieu Le Roi. Consequently the train was stopped in mid-section between telephones, the locomotive uncoupled and run forward to replenish its tanks. Meanwhile the guard sprinted about a quarter of a mile back down the track to place detonators on the rails to warn the following train, which duly came to a halt behind the carriages of the abandoned train. The guard of the second train carried out a similar exercise to warn the driver of the following railcar.

With such a basic system the safety record of the *Vivarais* was very good. However, there were the occasional blemishes to this record. The most serious accidents occurred in 1937 and 1944. On 31st December 1937, a late-running train, delayed by snow, was attempting to regain lost time near Raucoules-Brossettes. On one of the many tight curves on this part of the line, Mallet 414 took one of the curves far in excess of the permitted speed and became derailed. The locomotive ended up on its side at the bottom of the embankment, its driver sustaining serious injuries. The baggage van immediately behind the locomotive was extensively damaged, while the four carriages were derailed but remained upright.

The most serious accident during the life of the *Réseau du Vivarais* occurred on 26th June 1944. A mixed train en route to La Voûte sur Loire stopped at Yssingeaux to collect extra wagons. This additional load resulted in the train being in excess of the permitted maximum of 90 tonnes for this section of the line. As a result, the ensemble approached the viaduct at Chavalamard at excessive speed, resulting in a major derailment. Most of the carriages and wagons left the track and plunged down into the ravine far below. Twelve passengers were killed and fifty-nine injured in the badly damaged coaches, some of which were reduced to nothing more than matchwood. This serious accident could not have occurred at a worse time for the *Vivarais*. Recent research suggests that on 5th July the advancing American Army inadvertently shelled the works complex at Le Cheylard, believing it to be a main line centre of value to the retreating Germans.

Even the preserved CFV has had one accident of note. On a particularly busy day, 14th June 1970, an extra railcar was pressed into service to cope with the large number of passengers. Due to an uncharacteristic breakdown in communications, two railcars suffered a head-on collision at Garnier. Three passengers were injured in the accident, whilst the two railcars suffered considerable damage.

3.1. **SLM Mallet No. 401 waits at Tence with a Monday morning freight in September 1959. The coaches were being returned empty after the weekend.** **(J.B. Snell).**

3.2. **A Billard A-150-D-2 stands at St. Agrève on 25th July 1966. There appears to be some bartering taking place alongside the leading car whilst other goods are being loaded into the luggage compartment. (J. L. Rochaix/BVA).**

3.3. **A busy period at Le Cheylard was recorded on 24thJuly 1966, as Mallet No.403 runs past the workshops where a number of Billard railcars are in attendance. (J. L. Rochaix/BVA).**

Prior to the introduction of the railcars in 1935, all trains were steam-hauled. The formation varied from passenger trains and heavy freight trains, invariably loaded with timber, to many mixed trains with vans and wagons carrying a variety of merchandise attached to the passenger carriages. Usually the goods vehicles were assembled immediately behind the locomotive, although there were often exceptions to this rule. After the introduction of the railcars, most of the passenger traffic was handled by these more nimble machines. However, the railcars were more limited in their passenger capacity and at busy periods steam-hauled passenger trains continued to run - mainly mixed trains. Even the railcars often ran with a small parcels van attached to the rear.

As already mentioned, the steam locomotives continued to haul the heavy freight trains exclusively until the 1960s, when they were joined by a diesel hydraulic, which was acquired to supplement the, by then, dwindling stud of Mallets. Since the late 1940s many of the lighter freight trains, particularly on the easier-graded sections of the system, had been hauled by small diesel locomotives constructed by the CFD from withdrawn steam locomotives. In addition to the heavy freight trains, the Mallets were of considerable use during the winter months, when the snow lay deep on the higher parts of the route. With snowploughs attached to the Mallet front buffer beams, many of the passenger trains reverted to steam haulage, whilst it was not unknown for a snowbound railcar to be assisted by a Mallet, which presented a somewhat bizarre sight.

The aforementioned busy periods, when steam-hauled mixed trains ran, were largely in connection with market and fair days at towns such as Lamastre and Tence. Normally these trains ran early in the morning. For example, the Lamastre Fair Day train departed from Le Cheylard at 5.45am, returning during the early afternoon. One genuine timetabled steam-hauled passenger train survived

3.4.   Lamastre in its heyday, a scene of much activity in 1954. The locomotive is SLM Mallet No. 406. (F. Collardeau/CFTM).

until 1968. This ran between June and August on Sundays and Fête Days, and in one direction only, from St Agrève to Dunières. The reason for its existence was due to the many inhabitants of St Etienne and the surrounding area who ventured to the hills of the Massif. They all trickled out during the weekend by various railcars but the majority wished to return at the same time. This entailed producing a train far in excess of the capacity of a railcar even with two trailer coaches in tow. The train left St Agrève at 6.50pm, arriving at Dunières at 8.05pm, where the passengers crossed to the SNCF station to continue their journey home. The empty coaches were worked back to St Agrève early on the following Monday morning, the entire ensemble being "put to bed" for another week.

Apart from these exceptions, the CFD ran an efficient and economic service on the *Vivarais* system for seventy-eight years. The advent of the railcars in 1935 revolutionised the passenger services, providing a fast and reliable means of transport between the valleys of the Loire and Rhône.

Although the various railway systems in the CFD group were operated independently of each other, there was one notable exception. The *CFD Lozère*, which was about fifty miles south in the Cevénnes, was operated by the *Vivarais* management, the *Lozère* services being included in the *Vivarais* timetable. The *CFD Lozère* ran for thirty miles from Florac to Ste Cécile d'Andorge, and was yet another highly scenic journey. Steam traction was abandoned in 1954 but a limited railcar service continued until 1968. The line closed at the same time as the *Vivarais*. As will be seen from the forthcoming chapters, there were numerous cases of locomotives and railcars being transferred from Le Cheylard to Florac to assist the smaller railway. Many of these transfers were for a relatively short period, whilst others were on a permanent basis.

Reference was made above to the timetable. In the 1960s this included, naturally, the three surviving arms of the *Vivarais*, Le Cheylard-Dunières, Le Cheylard-La Voulte sur Rhône and Le Cheylard-Tournon, plus the aforementioned Lozère service. In addition it included the bus service from Le Puy to Dunières which had replaced the closed section of line between La Voûte sur Loire and Dunières.

3.5   Mallet No. 406 was photographed shunting timber wagons at Lamastre in August 1959. (J. B. Snell).

CHAPTER FOUR

STEAM LOCOMOTIVES OF THE VIVARAIS

The *Réseau du Vivarais* was renowned for its use of Mallet-type locomotives throughout its existence, although they were supplemented by a number of smaller machines of conventional design. Before describing the various classes of locomotive that the CFD acquired for use on the system, a brief history of the Mallet design follows as an introduction.

Anatole Mallet [1837-1919], born in Geneva, was an engineer who will be remembered for his development of compounding and the articulated locomotives that bear his name. Mallet patented his own system of compounding in 1874 and two years later his first three locomotives were constructed. These were modest 0-4-2T two cylinder cross-compound machines built by Schneider for the Bayonne and Biarritz Railway. These small locomotives were followed by further single-unit cross-compounds built by various manufacturers for use in France, Germany and Russia. It was not until 1884 that Mallet took out his patent for articulated locomotives incorporating his compound theories. Unlike other articulated designs, such as Fairlie and Meyer, Mallets were, in fact, semi-articulated locomotives. They comprised a conventional rigid power unit at the rear, with an articulated power unit at the front. It was the secondary narrow gauge lines with light track, sharp curves and steep gradients for which the design was intended. Unlike the Fairlie and Meyers, which initially suffered from keeping the high pressure joints on their power bogies steam-tight, Mallet's design overcame the problem by using low pressure steam through the moving joints. The high pressure cylinders were confined to the rear rigid units, whilst the low pressure cylinders were fitted to the front bogie units. With such a design the hp steam pipes were brought from the dome to the high pressure cylinders without need for any moving joints. The exhaust pipes from the hp cylinders to the larger lp cylinders on the front truck required a swivel joint at the same location as the swivel pin for the bogie unit, whilst the exhaust pipes from the lp cylinders to the blast pipe required a further swivel joint to counter the relative movement between the smokebox and bogie unit frame. This basic design was used throughout Europe, with the notable exception of Great Britain, on narrow gauge lines, particularly in France, Switzerland, Germany, Spain and Portugal, until the decline of steam in the 1960s.

It was in the USA that the Mallet design was taken to its ultimate limits. Having perfected high pressure steam joints, the American constructors, such as ALCO, Lima and Baldwin, produced large numbers of simple expansion Mallets of gigantic proportions, capable of hauling enormous freight trains of considerable length and weight. The ultimate development was achieved in 1941 when ALCO introduced the 4-8-8-4 "Big Boys" for the Union Pacific Railroad. These 133ft monsters, weighing 535 tons, were the largest steam locomotives ever built. However, the final vindication of Anatole Mallet's theories came with the development by the Norfolk and Western Railroad of their Y6B 2-8-8-2 compound locomotives introduced in 1948. These were slightly smaller than the "Big Boys", weighing 442 tons and about 10ft shorter in overall length.

In addition to the *Vivarais*, the other notable examples of metre gauge Mallets in France were to be found on the *Réseau Breton, PO Corrèze, CFD Lozère* and in Corsica. The majority were of 0-4-4-0T configuration until the prototype 0-6-6-0T design was delivered to the *Vivarais* in 1902. The largest of the French Mallets were the eight *Réseau Breton* 0-6-6-0Ts built by Piguet in 1914, whilst the credit for the last to be constructed lies with the SACM who built the last four for the *Vivarais* in 1932.

SACM 0-4-4-0T Mallets - Nos 45-48 & 63-64

In 1885 a set of drawings for an 0-4-4-0 design by Anatole Mallet was displayed at the Antwerp Exhibition. This design was for a locomotive with a low axle load to suit secondary railways.

4.1.   SACM 0-4-4-0T No.63 is pictured at Yssingeaux in 1946. This was the last survivor of the original batch   of Mallets supplied to the CFD in 1890/1. Its final years were spent working on the La Voûte-Raucoules line until its closure in 1952. (Coll. Dr. Brenot/BVA).

The first customer for such a machine was Paul Decauville, who required a 60cm gauge example with an axle load of 3 tonnes. The resulting machine, weighing a mere 11 tonnes, was built by *Ateliers Metallurgiques* at Tubize in 1887 and underwent successful trials at Decauville's works at Petit-Bourg near Paris.

The following year the *Société Alsacienne* [SACM] at Belfort built a prototype 24-tonne metre gauge example of the same design for the CFD. This first metre gauge Mallet [CFD No 42] was despatched to the Seine and Marne line, where it proved to be a great success. With the initial section of the *Réseau du Vivarais* between La Voûte sur Loire and Yssingeaux under construction, locomotives of the same design as No 42 were deemed to be ideal for the steeply graded line. Consequently, four locomotives, Nos 45-48, were constructed in 1890 at Belfort. The following year two more, Nos 63 and 64, were delivered for use on the Tournon-Lamastre line. Both Nos 45 and 64 were initially tested on the Seine and Marne prior to being despatched to the *Vivarais.*

These fairly small locomotives were built to the 1885 Antwerp drawings and became a SACM and Tubize standard design. Examples could be found as far afield as France, Germany, Switzerland, Corsica, Algeria and Indo-China. Principal dimensions were as follows: dry weight 19 tonnes [24 tonnes in working order]; wheel diameter 3ft; wheelbase 13ft; overall length 25ft; hp cylinders 9¾ in diameter; lp cylinders 15in diameter; boiler diameter 3¼ ft; boiler tubes 89 in total, 11ft in length. With their Belpaire boilers, these machines were a very advanced design, capable of hauling loads of 100 tonnes up a gradient of 1 in 250.

The six locomotives gave excellent service to the *Réseau du Vivarais*, mainly on the lighter freight trains, although they were somewhat eclipsed by the larger machines that appeared after 1902. After the completion of the full system, they were mainly confined to the less steeply graded sections, although they could be found operating on their original "stamping ground", the La Voûte line, until their withdrawal. No 48 was transferred permanently to the *CF Provence* in 1943, whilst No 64 was loaned to the *Lozère* between 1916 and 1919. No 63 was the last to be withdrawn from service, in 1946, although it remained in store until 1955 when it was "put out to grass" at Raucoules-Brossettes until the mid-1960s.

Regrettably, none of these historically important locomotives has survived. However, two later but similar, albeit heavier, machines, built in 1906 by Blanc-Misseron for the *PO Corrèze* have been preserved and can be found on the two surviving sections of the *Vivarais*.

4.2. **The last surviving Fives-Lille 2-6-0T was No.61. It is shunting at Le Cheylard on 4[h] August 1954. (F. Collardeau).**

Fives-Lille 2-6-0T; Nos 57-62

In 1891 the two relatively lightly graded lines from La Voulte sur Rhône-Le Cheylard and Tournon-Lamastre were completed. It was considered that locomotives of a more conventional type would be suitable for these sections although, as already mentioned, two of the SACM Mallets were drafted to Tournon for use on the heavier trains. Since 1889 the CFD had been using 2-6-0Ts of a standard design on most of its lines, examples being built by various French locomotive constructors.

The six locomotives Nos 57-62 were built by Fives-Lille and delivered between May and August 1891. Nos 57-60 were despatched initially to Tournon, whilst 61 and 62 went to Le Cheylard. After completion of the entire network in 1903, these useful machines could be found on the whole system, although Le Cheylard-La Voulte was their usual place of work in later years. Rather surprisingly these 2-6-0 tank engines were heavier than the SACM 0-4-4-0 Mallet tanks. Their principal dimensions were: dry weight 23tonnes [29 tonnes in working order]; coupled wheel diameter 3ft 3ins; leading wheel diameter 31ins; wheelbase 14ft; overall length 25ft; cylinder diameter 9¾ ins; boiler tubes 131. The boiler diameter and tube length is unrecorded, but judging by the number of tubes, the boilers were obviously larger than those of the small Mallets.

4.3.   No.61 awaits its fate at St. Julien Boutières, along with other withdrawn stock in September 1958. (J. B. Snell).

No 62 was transferred to the *CFD Charentes* in western France in 1914, never to return. Nos 57, 58 and 60 were withdrawn from stock prematurely in 1944, having been severely damaged in the bombardment at Le Cheylard in July that year. In fact, 57 and 60 were already stored out of use at that time. No 59 remained in service until 1948, whilst the last survivor was retained for light duties until 1957 and tantalisingly remained in store at St Julian-Boutières until 1965. What a pity it did not survive a further three years, as surely it would be a historic and useful asset to the CFV operation.

Although none of the *Vivarais* Fives-Lille 2-6-0Ts has survived, an example of the same design, built by Cail in 1895, is to be found in the museum at Pithiviers. This was No 77 of the aforementioned *CFD Charentes* line. The design was very compact, with large water tanks extending to the front extremity of the smokebox, resulting in a somewhat square appearance. In common with the SACM Mallets, Salter safety valves were fitted behind the dome, which was situated on the front ring of the boiler barrel. A sand dome was placed on the rear section of the boiler. As built, the cabs were very spartan, with completely open sides above the tank level, although fitted with both front and rear plates with oblong spectacle windows. In due course the *Vivarais* locomotives were fitted with upper cab sides to offer the crews some protection from the elements. The Cail-built example at Pithiviers is, however, preserved in its original condition, complete with brass domes and a bell.

Pinguely 0-6-0Ts; Nos 81-83

When the final links of the *Réseau du Vivarais* were being built in 1902, an urgent need arose for some small locomotives for use on construction trains. By good fortune, three 0-6-0 tank engines were being built at that time at the Pinguely works in Lyon. These locomotives were intended for use on the *CF d'Indre et Loire*, west of Orleans. However, the CFD stepped in and despatched them to Le Cheylard upon completion, no doubt ordering replacement engines for Indre at the same time.

These fairly small locomotives had a dry weight of 17 tonnes [21½tonnes in working condition], wheel diameter of 3ft, wheelbase a mere 7ft, overall length 22ft and cylinder diameters of 12ins. Once again, boiler dimensions are unrecorded apart from the number of tubes, which totalled 121. As on the Fives-Lille machines, the side tanks extended to the front of the smokebox, although they lacked the somewhat square appearance of the earlier design. The cabs were more commodious than those of the 2-6-0Ts, although they were open-backed in common with many locomotives of the period.

Their life on the *Vivarais* was very short. No 83 stayed only six months, being transferred to the *CF Seine et Marne* in November 1902. Nos 81 and 82 fared a little better before beginning a nomadic existence through the CFD empire in 1909. No 81 finally found a permanent home at the *CFD Lozère* in 1930, whilst No 82 was transferred to the *CF Dordogne* at around the same time.

Fortunately three examples of these delightful machines have survived into preservation. No 101, built in 1904 for the *CF Morbihan* in the far west of France, near Nantes, now works on the *CF La Baie de Somme* on the Channel coast between Calais and Dieppe. Sister engine No 103, also from the *CF Morbihan*, now stands on a plinth near the river at Tournon, alongside a statue of Marc Seguin. Also at Tournon and in use on lightly-loaded trains on the CFV, is a twin-cab example of the same design. This 1909-built locomotive was No 31 of the *Tramway Ouest Dauphiné* and is one of two surviving twin-cab machines still in use in France.

SLM 0-6-6-0T; Mallets Nos 401-408

With the completion of the *Vivarais* system in 1903, incorporating long gradients of up to 1 in 30 and many reverse curves, it was obvious that large powerful yet flexible locomotives would be required. At that time the French railway industry was enjoying a boom period and all the locomotive manufacturers' workshops were flooded with orders. Unable to find a company in France willing to undertake the design and construction at the time, the CFD turned to the *Schweizerische Lokomotiv und Maschinenfabrik* [SLM] at Winterthur in Switzerland. The SLM already had experience of building Mallets, having constructed twelve such machines for the *Rhätische Bahn* [RhB] between 1896 and 1902.

The CFD requirement for the *Vivarais* was for something larger and the resulting 0-6-6-0Ts were the first locomotives of that wheel arrangement in the world. The prototype No 401 was delivered in February 1902, followed by 402-405 the following year. The final batch, Nos 406-408, arrived in 1905. Immediately these eight locomotives became known as the classic *Vivarais* type. With their low-slung boilers topped by a typically Swiss flared chimney, adorned by the locomotive numbers in brass figures, and long flat-topped side tanks, they were truly handsome machines. Their dry weight was 37 tonnes [44 tonnes in working order], wheel diameter 3ft 4ins, and total wheelbase of 21ft [although the wheelbase of each power unit was only 7ft 3ins]; total length 36ft, hp cylinders of 12 ¼ins diameter, lp cylinders 16in diameter. Boiler diameter was a fraction under 4ft, with 152 tubes, 12ft in length and a working pressure of 210lbs per square inch. The prototype was tested upon delivery and successfully hauled a 160-tonne train up a 1 in 34 gradient near Yssingeaux.

4.4.   This is an almost timeless view of SLM Mallet No.403 at Tournon on 2nd September 1962. The spark arrestor is the more common variant used by the CFD during periods of hot and dry weather. (J. L. Rochaix/BVA).

As built, the SLM locomotives had Salter safety valves on the front of the steam dome, whilst the sand dome was situated at the rear above the front of the firebox. In due course this arrangement was modified, the Salter valves being replaced by Pop safety valves above the firebox and the sand dome moved to a forward position on the boiler. The hp cylinders had rounded tops fitted with piston valves, whilst the large lp cylinders, with their long piston rod covers protruding from the front, were fitted with slide valves and consequently were more square in design. The cranked axle on each power unit was on the rear pair of wheels, which resulted in long connecting rods to the valve gear and pistons. When seen in action, these long rods accentuate the length of these impressive machines. The steam ejector pipe for the vacuum brake system was fed along the top of the right hand tank and up the side of the chimney. The two surviving working locomotives, 403 and 404, were for a time modified with the ejector pipe routed up the side of the steam dome, as on the later SACM-built machines. During a recent overhaul No 403 had this modification reversed, and once again a copper pipe is fed up the side of the shapely flared chimney.

With two exceptions, all eight of the SLM Mallets spent their entire working lives on the *Réseau du Vivarais*, hauling both freight and passenger trains. The two exceptions were 408, which was transferred to the *CF Lozère* between 1909 and 1911, whilst 406 spent eighteen months between January 1944 and June 1945 working on the *CF Provence*.

At the end of World War II many of the locomotives were in a very poor state of repair and were sent away for major overhauls at the *Depot de La Capelette*, near Marseille. During the course of these overhauls Nos 401, 404, 405 and 408 were fitted with modified cabs incorporating a small coal bunker. This bunker was so small that the increased fuel capacity could not have been of much

4.5.   Mallet No.405 simmers at Le Cheylard in 1953. Note the very basic type of spark arrestor fitted to the shapely flared chimney.   (Photo. M. Rifault - Coll. J. L. Rochaix/BVA)

advantage, most of the briquettes still being stacked on the cab floor in the time-honoured fashion.

With the exception of 402, which was withdrawn in 1942 (but not scrapped until 1955), the remaining members of the class continued in service until the later years of the CFD operation. By 1965 only 403 and 404 remained in service and, as recorded in Chapter One, were officially retained for emergency use. However, their presence was soon noted throughout the enthusiast movement and many "last steam-hauled" excursions were run - invariably hauled by 403, which the CFD had repainted green in place of the standard CFD black. This revised colour scheme gave the Swiss-built locomotive even more of a Swiss appearance, being approximately the same shade of green as the surviving RhB steam locomotives.

When the CFTM (the operating company of the CFV) took over the operation of the Tournon-Lamastre line in 1969, Nos 403 and 404 were the first locomotives to be transferred to the new organisation. Both locomotives were in turn sent away for repair at the workshops of the *CFTA de Gray*, near Dijon, in the early 1970s, since when they have continued in service on the CFV. No 403 had a further overhaul at Tournon in 1994 following a period out of use. The pioneer, No 401, which had been withdrawn in 1966 following two years in store, was purchased, in poor condition, by the CFTM. For the last twenty five years or so it has stood, rusty and partially dismantled, in the yard at Tournon, being robbed for spare parts to keep its sister locomotives working. Many of its components were used in the recent overhaul of 403, but it is hoped eventually to restore this historic locomotive to working order.

Fives-Lille Prototype 2-6-2T; No 251

In 1906 the CFD uncharacteristically took delivery of a locomotive which was quite unsuitable for use on the *Vivarais*. This two- cylinder compound 2-6-2T was intended for lighter passenger trains. With a wheelbase of 20ft 6ins and 3ft 6in driving wheels, it obviously did not agree with the numerous reverse curves and steep gradients. The other principal dimensions were: total length 31ft; dry weight 33 tonnes [37 tonnes in working order]; hp cylinder 14½ ins and lp cylinder 18½ ins - obviously a fairly large machine. Unfortunately the boiler dimensions are unrecorded apart from the fact that it had 144 tubes.

This sprightly locomotive proved to be ideal for its intended purpose on a length of reasonably straight track, something which was virtually unknown on the *Réseau du Vivarais*. The service of 251 on the system lasted exactly three years, during which period it worked occasional trains on the lightly graded Le Cheylard-La Voulte sur Rhône line. In June 1909 this interesting locomotive was transferred to the *CFD Lozère*, a line for which it was far more suitable, particularly with much lighter trains.

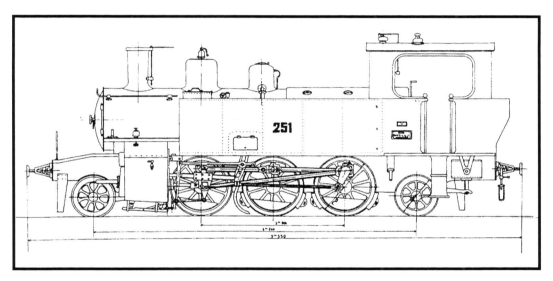

4.6.   This is the Fives-Lille Compound 2-6-2T No. 25l which evaded the attention of photographers during its short sojourn on the Vivarais. This drawing depicts the low pressure side with its large cylinder. (Coll. J .F. Organ).

SACM 2-4-4-0T Mallets; Nos 321-323

After the unsuccessful trials with 251 on the lighter passenger trains, the CFD once again turned their attention to Mallet locomotives for these duties. In 1908 they acquired a trio of 2-4-4-0Ts from SACM, Nos 321, 322 and 323, whilst a further two were built at the same time and despatched to the *CFD Lozère*. These were fairly compact machines with a dry weight of 30 tonnes [38 tonnes in working order]. Coupled wheels were 3ft 4ins diameter and the leading wheels 2ft 6ins. Wheelbase was 21ft 6ins and the total length 32 ft. Hp cylinders were 9¼in diameter and the lp cylinders 14 ins. The boiler diameter was 3ft 6ins with 134 tubes, 10ft 6ins in length. The locomotives developed a tractive effort of 8,140lbs.

Compared to the 2-6-2T, they were far more suited to the work intended for them. However, No 323 only stayed for three years, being transferred to the *Lozère* in September 1911. Nos 321 and

4.7. SACM 2-4-4-0T Mallet No. 321 stands at Yssingeaux in 1946. According to the records this loco-motive had been withdrawn from service the previous year but obviously had been returned to duty on the La Voûte line. (Coll. Dr. Brenot/BVA).

322 remained, working mainly from Le Cheylard to either Tournon or La Voulte. Both locomotives spent periods elsewhere. Between 1916 and 1919 they were both sent on loan to the *Réseau Meusien* for the battle of Verdun, whilst at the latter end of World War II they were despatched to the *CF Provence* from January 1944 to June 1945. Immediately after their return 322 was transferred to the *Lozère* - never to return. No 321 remained at Le Cheylard stored out of use as, of course, by this time the type of traffic for which they were intended was now being handled by the fleet of railcars. No 321 was finally withdrawn from stock in 1953, when it was "put out to grass" at Raucoules-Brossettes along with other redundant locomotives.

SACM 0-6-6-0T; Mallets Nos 409-414

Following the introduction of the three 2-4-4-0T Mallets, Nos 321-323, in 1908, the locomotive fleet of the *Réseau du Vivarais* was to remain static for the next nineteen years. However, by 1926 it was apparent that the increasingly heavy freight trains were beyond the capabilities of the smaller locomotives. Consequently it was decided to purchase additional larger engines in the shape of more 0-6-6-0T Mallets. Unlike the situation in 1902, when the French locomotive industry was overwhelmed with orders, SACM were in a position to construct the new order. Two locomotives, Nos 409 and 410, were delivered in May 1927. The principal dimensions were identical to the SLM machines in respect of the power units, cylinders and wheels. The major difference was the boiler. This was higher pitched than the elegant low-slung Swiss design and was fitted with a Belpaire firebox. In contrast to the shapely flared chimney of the earlier machines, the new locomotives had a typically French stovepipe affair in conjunction with a Kylchap blastpipe. The water tanks were larger than on the older design, with sloping tops at their front ends. Dry weight was the same as the SLM locomotives [37 tonnes] but slightly heavier in working order. Tractive effort was the same for

4.8. One of the 1909 built SACM 2-4-4-0T Mallets that was supplied to the CFD Lozère, No.325 stands at Florac in 1953. Note the lifting jack in front of the water tank. (J. L. Rochaix /BVA).

4.9. No. 410, one of the 1927 SACM 0-6-6-0T Mallets, is seen at St. Agrève in 1950. This view clearly illustrates the earlier design of cab fitted to the first two of these later locomotives. (J. Paillard/BVA).

both designs at 13,000lb.

In 1932 four more locomotives of the same type were delivered from SACM. Numbered 411-414, these differed in having an improved cab design incorporating a side window and an external coal bunker at the rear. These modifications gave these later engines an increased weight in working order of 45 tonnes. The 1932 batch gained their place in history as being the last metre gauge steam locomotives to be built in France.

Although the SACM locomotives worked alongside the earlier SLM machines, the latter were more popular with the crews. The higher centre of gravity of the later engines caused them to feel less stable on the *Vivarais* track with super elevation on the many curves which varied between

4.10. No. 411, the first of the 1932 batch of SACM Mallets was photographed at Dunières in 1946. This rear view shows the later cab design incorporating an external bunker and side windows. Also seen are the two vacuum cylinders beneath the bunker.
(Coll. Dr. Brenot/ BVA).

very excessive to almost non-existent. As a result, despite working fairly modest mileages compared with their older sisters, they were outlived in service by three of the SLM locomotives.

Nos 409 and 410 were transferred to the *Lozère* in 1932, shortly after the delivery of the last four locomotives, not returning until 1942 and 1945 respectively. With the exception of 413 and 414, the whole class had been put into store by 1951 and finally withdrawn in 1955. Fortunately the final two members of the class continued in service until 1962 and, although officially withdrawn in 1965, they were still in store at Le Cheylard at the time of closure in 1968. This fortunate state of affairs resulted in the CFTM purchasing these two historic locomotives for use on the CFV. No 414 was restored to working order at *CFTA de Gray* in 1972, while 413's restoration was a more prolonged affair. Work began at the *CFTA* workshops but was delayed due to other commitments. The rebuild was finally completed at Knittelfeld in Austria and 413 eventually entered service on the CFV in 1986, proudly bearing the name *Marc Seguin* on its cab sides.

Despite their unpopularity in earlier years, 413 and 414 have handled the majority of the traffic on the Tournon-Lamastre line during the last decade. With the improved track of the preserved line, the tendency for these later machines to roll on curves has been eliminated, and the SACM Mallets have become firm favourites with both crews and public alike.

Proposed 0-6-6-0T Mallets for the Le Cheylard-Aubenas extension

When plans for the ambitious scheme to build a 30-mile line over the mountains were being made in 1920, it was obvious that additional locomotives would be required. A company previously not involved with CFD motive power requirements, Schneider and Company of Creusot, submitted drawings for an enlarged version of the SLM machines. As in the case of the later SACM Mallets, the principal dimensions of the proposed locomotives were identical to the Swiss machines apart from a larger boiler. Dry weight would have been 38½ tonnes and 48 tonnes in working order. In appearance they would have been virtually identical with the SLM locomotives and would have been numbered 501-510.

With the failure of the Le Cheylard-Aubenas scheme to materialise, the locomotives never progressed further than the initial drawing stage. It is perhaps surprising that the design was not revived when additional motive power was required in 1927, rather than purchasing the excellent SACM locomotives.

The Vivarais locomotives in service

In common with most railways in France, the *Vivarais* locomotives used briquettes as fuel - literally bricks made from compressed coal dust. These were supplemented by a quantity of slack coal, the combination of the two producing large amounts of brown smoke which lingered in the atmosphere long after the train had passed.

During periods of dry weather the chimneys were fitted with wire mesh spark arrestors of a very basic design. In appearance they were similar to a domestic house chimney cowl and their efficiency is somewhat doubtful. Until the early 1970s, in the first years of the preservation era, the CFV continued to fit them to the locomotives during the dry summer months. However, they ceased to be fitted after fuel from another source was obtained, and also the firemen improved their firing techniques. This change of fuel coincided with a smoking ban being put into effect on all trains and no trouble with lineside fires has been experienced since. Whether it was the change of fuel, the improved firing techniques or the smoking ban which prevented the fires is a matter of conjecture.

All the locomotives were fitted with typically French high-pitched whistles which sound so much in character with the engines and the terrain they worked in. Vacuum braking was used on the steam locomotives, unlike the railcars which were air-braked. Right hand drive was standard, whilst invariably the two crew members were separated by a stack of briquettes on the cab floor. The large Mallets were fitted with flange lubricators in order to minimise wear to the wheels on the multitude of curves on the system. Despite the provision of these lubricators, there was still a certain amount of wheel squealing to be heard on the sharper curves. As with most metre gauge lines, centre buffers were used with adjustable chainlink couplings on each side.

During the winter months, when snow lay almost permanently on the higher parts of the route, large wedge-shaped snowploughs were fitted to the front of the locomotives. These were sufficiently effective in clearing a path for the train service to run throughout the year. Very rarely was the line closed due to the snow being too deep to penetrate.

With so many locomotives of two similar classes, interchanging of parts was not unknown. With the SLM Mallets [401-408] and the SACM version [409-414] sharing identical power units, parts were also distributed between the two types. For example, 403 is currently fitted with the wheels from 409, while 413 has a number of components stamped 401 among its valve gear.

When retired from active service, the steam locomotives were usually stored for a considerable period at various locations, mainly Le Cheylard, Dunières or Tournon, until finally being withdrawn. Even then they weren't always cut up for scrap immediately but "put out to grass" elsewhere on the railway. St Julien Boutières and Raucoules-Brossettes were particularly well known locations for derelict locomotives. In May 1965, for instance, the situation was as follows: 413 was stored at Tournon and clearly hadn't moved for months; at Le Cheylard 401 and 414 were dead and rusty behind the shed, 404 was inside the shed, while 403 was being re-tubed inside the workshop. At St Julien Nos 405, 406, 407, 409 and 61 were all derelict, whilst at Raucoules Nos 63, 321, 410 and 412 were in a similar condition. The latter had possibly been there since the La Voûte line closed in 1952. Also at Raucoules was another locomotive in the shed - possibly, by deduction, 408.

At around that time it was reported that the *Domaines*, a French equivalent to the Ministry of Supply, were to auction on 19th June 1965, at Le Puy *Locomotive SLM No 408 of 1905 and four locomotive wrecks.* This would appear to be the collection stored at Raucoules, but the *Domaines* involvement remains a mystery.

4.11. Preserved SLM Mallet No.403 was recorded at Tournon on 29th August 1996 while being prepared for its next turn of duty. (J. F. Organ).

4.12. SACM Mallet No.414 is on shed at Le Cheylard in September 1958. This was the last steam locomotive to be supplied to the CFD Vivarais and it arrived in 1932. (J. B. Snell).

CFD VIVARAIS STEAM LOCOMOTIVES

0-4-4-0T MALLET SACM BELFORT 1890/91

CFD No.	WORKS No.	DELIVERY	STORED	WITHDRAWN	NOTES
45	4206	DEC 1890 (Ex S&M)	1937	1943	
46	4207	OCT 1890	1937	1943	
47	4208	OCT 1890	1945	1949	
48	4209	OCT 1890			To PROVENCE 1943
63	4274	AUG 1891	1946	1955	
64	4275	DEC 1891 (Ex S&M)	1941	1949	LOZÈRE 1916-19

2-6-0T FIVES-LILLE 1891

CFD No.	WORKS No.	DELIVERY	STORED	WITHDRAWN	NOTES
57	2721	MAY 1891	1942	1949	
58	2722	MAY 1891	1944	1949	
59	2723	MAY 1891	1948	1956	
60	2724	MAY 1891	1943	1949	
61	2725	AUG 1891	1957	1965	
62	2726	AUG 1891			To CHARENTES DEC 1914

0-6-0T PINGUELY 1902

CFD No.	WORKS No.	DELIVERY	DISPOSAL
81	112	MAR 1902	TO LOZÈRE JUNE 1909, MEUSIEN SOMME, VIVARAIS 1923-28, TRAMWAY ARDECHE 1928-1930, LOZÈRE MAR 1930 TO WITHDRAWAL.
82	113	MAR 1902	TO LOZÈRE FEB 1909, MEUSIEN SOMME, SAONE & LOIRE, ARDÈCHE, LOZÈRE, DORDOGNE APR 1942 TO WITHDRAWAL
83	114	MAR 1902	TO SEINE & MARNE NOV 1902

0-6-6-0T MALLET SLM WINTERTHUR 1901 - 05

CFD No.	WORKS No.	DELIVERY	STORED	WITHDRAWN	NOTES
401	1406	FEB 1902	1964	1966	TO CFV 1973
402	1491	MAR 1903	1942	1955	
403	1492	MAR 1903			TO CFV 1969
404	1493	APR 1903			TO CFV 1969
405	1494	MAY 1903	1954	1965	
406	1671	DEC 1905	1960	1965	PROVENCE 1944-45
407	1672	DEC 1905	1961	1965	
408	1673	DEC 1905	1962	1964	LOZÈRE 1909-11

2-6-2T FIVES-LILLE 1906

CFD No.	WORKS No.	DELIVERY	DISPOSAL
251	3272	JUNE 1906	TO LOZÈRE JUNE 1909

2-4-4-0T MALLET SACM BELFORT 1908

CFD No.	WORKS No.	DELIVERY	STORED	WITHDRAWN	NOTES
321	5820	AUG 1908	1945	1953	MEUSIEN 1916-19 PROVENCE 1944-45
322	5821	AUG 1908			MEUSIEN 1916-19 PROVENCE 1944-45 LOZÈRE 1945 -
323	5822	SEP 1908			TO LOZÈRE 1911

0-6-6-0T MALLET SACM GRAFFENSTADEN 1927/1932

CFD No.	WORKS No.	DELIVERY	STORED	WITHDRAWN	NOTES
409	7445	MAY 1927	1948	1955	LOZÈRE 1932-42
410	7446	MAY 1927	1950	1955	LOZÈRE 1932-45
411	7626	APR 1932	1947	1955	
412	7627	APR 1932	1951	1955	
413	7628	APR 1932	1962	1965	TO CFV 1969
414	7629	APR 1932	1962	1965	TO CFV 1972

CHAPTER FIVE

RAILCARS AND DIESEL LOCOMOTIVES

Railcars, or Autorails as they are known on their home soil, became a standard form of transport on French railways of all gauges during the 1930s. Many of these were built by companies whose names were synonymous with the automobile industry. De Dion Bouton and Renault both became involved, whilst the most impressive were designed and built by the legendary name of Bugatti. Designed in 1930, the Bugatti railcars built for the PLM were fitted with multiples of either two or four 15-litre 8-cylinder Type 41 *La Royale* petrol engines. One of the larger four-engined examples broke the railspeed record in 1933 when driven by Jean Bugatti at 122 mph. The wedge-shaped frontal design of these very advanced machines was the inspiration behind Sir Nigel Gresley's design for his A4 streamlined Pacifics.

The diesel-engined railcars produced for the secondary railways were far more modest but excellent in all respects. As early as 1924 the CFD had tested a petrol-engined loco-tractor built by Thomson-Houston on various lines, including the *Vivarais*. This experimental machine was not a great success due to its being underpowered, but it was obvious that further development would result in machines far more suitable for the intended purpose. In 1929 a petrol-electric railcar built by Crochat was again tested briefly on the *Vivarais* before being transferred to Charentes, where it achieved more success. These trials led to the CFD adopting railcars for the majority of passenger trains throughout their network of lines. By 1935 the diesel engine had been developed to a point where it had become a viable form of power unit for such machines. This led to a large number of diesel-engined railcars being built during the years preceding World War II. Ultimately the *Vivarais* became as well known for its railcars as its Mallets, with a total fleet of seventeen units. These comprised five De Dion Bouton and twelve Billard. The latter were of three types, A-150D, A-150-D-2 articulated twin units, and A-80-D. The four A-80-Ds, although built in 1937, did not arrive until 1951/2, when they were transferred from Charentes.

De Dion Bouton type ND; Nos 203-207

Five railcars were delivered from the works of the well known motor vehicle manufacturer, one of the oldest concerns of its type, in April 1935, with another two going to the *CFD Lozère*. These 30-seat units were powered by a 100hp 6-cylinder Mercedes engine built under licence by Unic. The power units were fitted directly above the front bogie wheels, to which traction was supplied via a 3-speed gearbox. The De Dions were handicapped by being single-ended and had to be turned at each end of their journeys. In appearance they resembled a contemporary single-decker bus, with a traditional style radiator at the front. Despite the inconvenience of being single-ended, the De Dion Boutons worked alongside the later Billards until the *Vivarais* closed in 1968. Nos 205 and 204 were transferred to the *Lozère* in 1947 and 1950 respectively, the former having been on loan to the associated line between 1938 and 1943.

The De Dion railcars were often to be seen hauling a small two-wheeled parcel truck, an open wagon with a tarpaulin sheet over a hooped frame providing protection for its contents. Six of these type NF trucks were built by De Dion, numbered 59-64. The six-wheeled type ND railcars were limited to 55kph [35mph] or 45kph [28mph] when hauling a parcel truck.

Five of the De Dion Boutons have survived in various conditions. No 207 is currently at Lamastre awaiting restoration to working order, having been acquired by the CFTM for the CFV operation in 1969. No 204 is in a similar condition at Tence, having worked on the CFR Dunières-St Agrève route during the early 1970s. No 206 and the two original Lozère units, 201 and 202, are also at Tence and Raucoules-Brossettes, but in a derelict state and unlikely to work again.

5.1. **De Dion Bouton Type ND Railcar No.207 waits at Le Cheylard in 1954. Unlike the later Billard machines, the De Dion examples were single ended and consequently had to be turned when they reached their destination.** **(M. Rifault/BVA).**

5.2. **De Dion Bouton No.204 pauses at Raucoules-Brossettes on 5th August 1948. At the rear is one or the type NF two wheeled parcel trucks. (F. Collardeau/BVA).**

Billard type A-150-D;Nos 211-214

Société Anonyme Billard of Tours were to become the most well known constructors of railcars, examples being found throughout France. A prototype was delivered in 1935 to the CFD for use on the Indre and Loire line, where it proved to be very successful. As a direct result of these initial trials, three similar vehicles, Nos 211-213, were delivered to the Vivarais in 1938, with a fourth, 214, following in 1940.

The 8-wheeled railcars, mounted on two bogies, were 46ft long and weighed 12½ tonnes. Seating capacity was forty-two plus a crew of two. There was a large baggage compartment immediately behind and alongside the engine compartment, which could carry over 2 tonnes of luggage and goods. Unlike the De Dions, they had driving controls at each end, which made them far more versatile in service.

Originally power was provided by a 150hp 6-cylinder diesel engine built by *Compagnie Lilloise de Moteurs [CLM]*. These proved to be not as reliable as had been hoped, and 214 was fitted with a Berliet motor of the same size when it was built in 1940. This too proved to be troublesome in service and the entire class was fitted with replacement engines built by *Willème* during the 1940s. These 150hp 6-cylinder power units proved to be far more successful and reliable in service.

The diesel engine was mounted above the leading bogie, drive to the wheels being taken via a 3-speed Minerva gearbox. A large radiator was fitted to the front of the vehicle whilst the exhaust system was mounted on the roof. The leading end driving position was in a fairly cramped cab alongside the bonnet enveloping the large diesel power unit. Due to the high radiator, the front windscreens were very small, which resulted in a fairly claustrophobic and, no doubt, very warm driving position. By contrast, the trailing end was controlled from a seat in the corner of the passenger compartment with a simple tubular bar between the driver and travellers.

5.3. Billard A-150-D No.211 is at Le Cheylard on 25th July 1966. No.211 along with 212, 223 and 224 was transferred to Provence in 1969. (J. L. Rochaix/ BVA).

The driving controls consisted of three gear levers, one for each gear, and the normal accelerator, brake and clutch pedals. Immediately in front of the driver was a wheel which to the uninitiated could be mistaken for a steering wheel. This, in fact, was the handbrake control which operated a magnetic shoe between the wheels on each bogie. When turned, this wheel lowered the shoes on to the track, providing a very effective parking brake. The distinctive twin-tone horns were operated by a lever on the dashboard, which was fitted with the usual instruments including a speedometer, fuel and temperature gauges.

5.4. Billard No.213 stands at St. Agrève in 1953. This view shows the rather ornate radiator grille incorporating the letters CFD which were originally fitted to these vehicles. (M. Rifault - Coll. J. L. Rochaix/BVA).

5.5. The trailing end of Billard A-150-D No. 214 is seen at Dunières in 1946. In contrast to the leading end, the driver had a much better view or the line when driving from the trailing end.
(Coll. Dr. Brenot/BVA)

5.6. Now we can examine the drivers controls in the leading end of Billard A-150-D No.213. Note the narrow windscreen and close proximity of the large Diesel engine. The three gear levers and handbrake wheel are also visible. (J. F. Organ).

Originally the radiators were protected by an ornate external grille incorporating the letters *CFD* in its design. These grilles were removed during the 1950s, resulting in a much improved appearance to the leading end. The trailing ends vaguely resembled the GWR railcars of the same vintage. Visibility for driver and passengers alike was excellent, and probably the best way to appreciate the scenic splendours of the *Vivarais* was to travel in the front seat of the trailing end of a Billard railcar.

No 214 spent six years between 1961 and 1967 on loan to the *Lozère* working alongside the fleet of De Dions on that line. After the *Vivarais* closed in 1968, Nos 211 and 212 were transferred to the *CF Provence* while 213 and 214 remained to be incorporated into the CFTM stock for the Tournon-Lamastre service. No 214 was involved in the aforementioned collision at Garnier in 1970, sustaining damage to its leading end. During repairs a modified radiator was fitted which was of less height than the original design. Improved technology allowed a smaller type to be efficient enough to provide adequate cooling for the Willème engine. The outcome of this modification, and the main reason for implementing it, was that deeper windscreens were fitted, allowing far better visibility for the driver.

Billard type A-80-D; Nos 313-316

These smaller railcars were built in 1937 and 1939 for use on the *CFD Charentes* line. When that railway closed in 1952 they were transferred to the *Vivarais*, 313 and 315 in fact arriving in 1951. Like the A-150-D series, they were mounted on two 4-wheeled bogies and weighed 9½ tonnes. They were 33ft long and carried thirty-two passengers plus crew. Power was originally supplied by a 90hp CLM engine which was subsequently replaced by a 100hp Willème diesel unit. In general design they were a scaled down version of the A-150-D machines. With the smaller power units, the driving compartment enjoyed better visibility due to the lower radiators allowing much deeper windscreens than on their larger sisters.

Following their arrival on the *Vivarais* they were extensively used on the lighter workings, and proved to be ideal for the purpose. No 314 spent seven years between 1954 and 1961 at the *CF Lozère*, returning there in 1967 until closure the following year. This well-travelled machine returned to Tournon in 1969 for use on the CFV where it has seen considerable use since that time. No 316 was also acquired by the CFTM for use on the CFV and was the other vehicle involved in the 1970 accident at Garnier. Following repair, 316 had many of its seats removed and was adapted for use by the permanent way department as their mobile track maintenance vehicle. Nos 313 and 315 went to the CFR in 1970, the former being used on occasional services on that line. It is currently at Dunières awaiting overhaul for use by the VFV organisation, whilst 315 has remained stored in a derelict condition at Tence.

5.8.   Billard A-80-D No.316 waits in the sun at Le Cheylard on 25th July 1966. Originally supplied to the CFD Charentes, these smaller machines were transferred to the Vivarais in 1951/2 when the former line closed.   (J.L. Rochaix/BVA).

5.9.   Billard No.316 departs from Le Cheylard towards St. Agrève in August 1959. Note the similarity in design features of the Billard and the A30 although the railcar predates the Austin by fifteen years. (J.B. Snell).

Billard articulated type A-150-D-2; Nos 221-224

Delivered in 1939, these four machines proved to be an excellent investment by the CFD. In appearance they were basically two A-80-D railcars permanently coupled together with their trailing end driving positions removed. They were mounted on three bogies, the centre one of which was positioned under both vehicles. Total length was 65ft, weight 16 tonnes, with a capacity of fifty-six passengers plus crew. Power was provided by a 150hp engine positioned in the rear of the leading car, drive via the 3-speed Minerva gearbox being taken to the centre bogie. As with the other Billard machines, the original CLM engines were replaced by 150hp Willème units early in their lives.

5.10. Billard A-150-D-2 No.222 stands alongside the Railcar and Rolling Stock shed at Le Cheylard on 24th July 1966. (J. L. Rochaix/BVA).

As originally designed, they were provided with two radiators, similar to those fitted to the A-80-D series, at each end of the combined units. In due course it was found that one radiator was adequate, as a result of which the trailing car radiator was removed and the vacated space blanked off. Bearing in mind that they were fitted with the larger 150hp engines, this says much for the efficiency of the smaller radiator - plus the fact that for much of the time it was at the trailing end of the double railcars, often with a trailer vehicle immediately behind it. The airflow surely could not have been too great in such circumstances. The return feed from the engine to the radiator header tank was taken over the roof and into the top of the radiator through a pipe which ran down the outside of the central windscreen. This feature was also adopted on A-150-D No 314 in its original condition.

No 221 worked briefly on the *CFD Indre et Loire* prior to its arrival at Le Cheylard. The remaining three were delivered direct from the works at Tours while 223 spent nine years between 1941 and 1950 at the small *CFD Yonne* in north-east France. In 1949 a short-lived attempt to generate additional traffic was introduced in the form of a non-stop service between La Voulte sur Rhône and Dunières. This was named *Flèche des Cévennes* and the articulated units were fitted with arrows on each vehicle, bearing the above name and obviously inspired by the *Golden Arrow*. The fact that the Cévennes were some miles south of the area in which the train operated adds to the mystique of this short-lived venture. The *CF Lozère* would have been a more appropriate location for a service of that name!

Following a decade in store, 221 was withdrawn in 1966 whilst the remaining three continued in service until closure in 1968. Nos 223 and 224 were then transferred to the *CF Provence* and 222 went to the CFR in 1970. Between that date and 1987, when that organisation ceased to operate, 222 handled the majority of the services between Dunières and St Agrève. This last survivor of these interesting articulated railcars was overhauled for use on the VFV between Dunières and Tence, and returned to service in 1997.

Additional vehicles for use with Billard railcars

Mention has already been made of the somewhat primitive parcel trucks built by De Dion Bouton for their railcars. However, Billards produced some far more sophisticated vehicles for use with their machines. These comprised passenger-carrying trailer cars and luggage vans.

In 1938 three Type R-210 trailer cars were delivered from Tours, Nos 1-3, and in 1952 a further three, numbers 11, 22 and 33, were transferred from Charentes along with the A-80-Ds. The R-210s were for all intents and purposes engineless A-80-D railcars and had a capacity of twenty-eight passengers, together with luggage or goods. The three ex-Charentes vehicles differed slightly in being fitted with toilets at the sacrifice of some luggage space.

For heavier goods items, three type RM luggage vans were also delivered from Charentes. They were wooden-bodied bogie vehicles with sliding doors and a capacity of 2 tonnes. In 1947 the CFD built a similar vehicle at Le Cheylard. This differed from the Billard RM series in that the bodywork was of steel and it ran on four wheels instead of two bogies. The capacity was the same as the earlier Billard-built examples. All these trailer vehicles were compatible with all the variations of Billard railcars. As mentioned earlier, the efficiency of the radiators must have been tested to its limits when the railcars were working with the trailing end leading and towing a trailer.

Some of these railcar trailer vehicles have survived. Three of the R-210 passenger cars, Nos 3, 11 and 22, are in service on the CFV while No 2 went to the CFR and is currently in store at Tence. One of the RM luggage vans, No 30, and the CFD-built No 40 are also in store at Tence, although their condition is very poor.

5.11.   Billard Type R-210 trailer car No.3 was at Lamastre on 23rd July 1966. These vehicles were basically engineless A-80-D units.
(J. L. Rochaix/BVA).

Diesel locomotives

As previously recorded, the CFD tested a petrol-electric loco-tractor built by Thomson-Houston in 1924 and a Crochat railcar in 1929. Their next involvement with the internal combustion engine occurred in 1930 when they acquired a small Petolat shunting tractor. This small machine was powered by a 12hp Daimler engine and worked on the *CF Saône et Loire* until 1954, when it was transferred to Le Cheylard. There it continued to perform light shunting duties until 1968, and it is now preserved at Lamastre. At present it is stored awaiting an overhaul and a return to working order.

5.12. CFD 0-6-0 Diesel Tractor X was found at Le Cheylard in 1961. This machine was built in 1949 from a 0-6-2T originally built in 1887 for the CFD L' Yonne by St. Léonard.
(M. Rifault – Coll J. L. Rochaix/BVA).

In 1947 a diesel-electric combined locomotive and luggage car built by Brissonneau and Lotz was tested on the *Vivarais* before being despatched to its final home on the Dakar-Niger Railway in West Africa. During its period on the *Vivarais* it successfully hauled heavy freight trains up the steep gradients, proving that diesel power was a force to be reckoned with.

During the years immediately following World War II, the CFD found itself with many small steam locomotives which were in a very rundown condition and not economically viable to overhaul. In 1948 the CFD workshops at Montmirail, fifty miles east of Paris, removed the boiler and other associated fittings from a Couillet 0-6-2T that had spent its working life on the *CFD Seine et Marne*. In place of the boiler was fitted a 180hp Willème diesel engine which drove the wheels via a Minerva 6-speed gearbox, resulting in a very powerful diesel shunting locomotive. Before returning

5.13. The small Pétolat shunting tractor was at work at Le Cheylard in September 1958.
(J. B. Snell).

5.14. CFD 0-6-0 Diesel Tractor Y was pictured at Le Cheylard on 19th June 1961. As with X, this machine was built at Le Cheylard in 1949 from a St. Léonard 0-6-2T. Note that Y has the cab at the extreme rear with a correspondingly longer bonnet.
(B. Roze/BVA).

5.15. CFD Bo-Bo Diesel Hydraulic locomotive No.040-003 stands at Le Cheylard on 8th May 1966.
(D. Trevor Rowe).

5.16. 040-003 is leaving the dual gauge SNCF section at St. Jean de Muzols 14th March 1964. Note that the metre gauge track diverges on an adverse camber.
(F. Collardeau).

5.17. Here is one of two small petrol engined inspection trollies built in 1932. Originally supplied to the CFD Charentes, they were transferred to the Vivarais in 1952. No.2 is seen at Le Cheylard on 2nd September 1962. (J. L. Rochaix/BVA).

to the *Seine et Marne*, No 852 spent six weeks at Le Cheylard for evaluation purposes. The following year, as a result of the successful testing of 852, the works at Le Cheylard were given the opportunity to produce two similar machines. Contrary to popular belief, the donor engines were not*Vivarais* 2-6-0Ts but a pair of 0-6-2Ts built by St Léonard in 1887 for the *CFD l'Yonne*. As with No 852, these two locomotives had their trailing wheels removed along with the boilers and fittings. The rolling chassis were fitted with the well-proven 180hp Willème units and hydraulic transmission. These two loco-tractors had no numbers but were referred to as X and Y and proved to be very versatile machines, equally at home shunting wagons or hauling the lighter freight trains, particularly on the La Voulte line. In 1960 another similar locomotive arrived from the *Seine et Marne*. This machine, No 13, was converted at Montmirail from a Couillet 0-6-0T built in 1883 for the *CFD Port Boulet-Chateaurenault*. Unlike X and Y, No 13 was fitted with a smaller Willème 150hp engine and was used for light shunting duties until 1968 when it was returned to Montmirail and ultimately scrapped.

The CFD built many of these diesel tractors from redundant steam locomotives. Two from the *CFD Lozère*, Nos 62 and 70, are currently preserved at Tence and are used to haul passenger trains on the VFV between Tence and Dunieres. Both X and Y have proved to be useful assets of the CFV since 1969 where, in addition to shunting, they have been used on the occasional passenger working between Tournon and Lamastre. Most of these interesting conversions featured a central cab behind a large "bullnose" bonnet and radiator. Y differs from the others in having its cab at the rear of the locomotive, resulting in a much longer bonnet, giving this particular machine a more imposing appearance.

In 1963 the works at Montmirail produced a number of genuine diesel-hydraulic Bo-Bo locomotives. Two of these went to the State-owned *PO Corrèze* while another pair went to Corsica. No 040-003 was despatched to Le Cheylard to work alongside the remaining Mallets on freight workings. This 32-tonne, 400hp machine, powered by two Poyaud 6-cylinder engines, proved to be a great success and in the final years hauled the majority of the heavy freight trains. These were large locomotives with a central cab similar in appearance to the numerous standard gauge DR units found throughout the former East Germany, a number of which were converted to metre gauge for use on the Harz system. Following the closure of the *Réseau du Vivarais* in 1968, 040-003 was transferred to the *CF Provence*, where it worked alongside its sisters from the *Corrèze* until 1974 when it was despatched to Corsica.

CFD RAILCARS

DE DION BOUTON TYPE ND 1935

CFD No.	WORKS No.	DELIVERY	NOTES AND DISPOSAL
203	121	APR 1935	WITHDRAWN 1953
204	122	APR 1935	To LOZÈRE 1950. CFR 1970. VFV 1992
205	123	APR 1935	To LOZÈRE 1938 - 43 and 1947 - 69
206	124	APR 1935	CFR 1970. VFV 1992
207	125	APR 1935	CFV 1969.

BILLARD TYPE A-150-D 1938/40

CFD No.	WORKS No.	DELIVERY	NOTES AND DISPOSAL
211	2007	MAY 1938	To PROVENCE 1969.
212	2008	MAY 1938	To PROVENCE 1969
213	2009	JUL 1938	To CFV 1969
214	2025	APR 1940	To LOZÈRE 1961-67. CFV 1969.

BILLARD TYPE A-150-D-2 1939

CFD No.	WORKS No.	DELIVERY	NOTES AND DISPOSAL
221	2022	APR 1939 (Ex I&L)	WITHDRAWN 1966 (In store since 1955)
222	2021	MAY 1939	To CFR 1970. VFV 1992.
223	2023	MAY 1939	To CFD YONNE 1941-50. PROVENCE 1969.
224	2024	JUN 1939	To PROVENCE 1969

BILLARD TYPE A-80-D 1937/9 (ALL Ex CFD CHARENTES)

CFD No.	WORKS No.	DELIVERY	NOTES AND DISPOSAL
313	1005	JUNE 1951	CFR 1970. VFV 1992.
314	1006	AUG 1952	To LOZÈRE 1954-61 and 1967-70 CFV 1970.
315	1024	MAY 1951	CFR 1970. VFV 1992.
316	1025	AUG 1952	CFV 1969.

RAILCAR TRAILERS AND LUGGAGE VANS

DE DION BOUTON TYPE NF LUGGAGE VANS 1935

CFD No.	WORKS No.	DELIVERY	NOTES AND DISPOSAL
59	59	APRIL 1935	CFR 1970. VFV 1992.
60	60	APRIL 1935	CFR 1970. VFV 1992.
61	61	APRIL 1935	To CFD LOZÈRE MAY 1938
62	62	APRIL 1935	To CFD LOZÈRE APRIL 1952
63	63	APRIL 1935	To CFD LOZÈRE APRIL 1952
64	64	APRIL 1935	To CFD LOZÈRE DEC 1959

BILLARD TYPE R-210 TRAILER CARS 1937/38

CFD No.	WORKS No.	DELIVERY	NOTES AND DISPOSAL
1	809	MAY 1938	To PROVENCE 1969.
2	810	JULY 1938	To CFR 1970. VFV 1992
3	811	JULY 1938	To CFV 1969
11	?/1937	AUG 1952 (Ex CHARENTES)	To CFV 1969
22	?/1937	AUG 1952 (Ex CHARENTES)	To CFV 1969
33	?/1937	AUG 1952 (Ex CHARENTES)	To PROVENCE 1969.

BILLARD TYPE RM LUGGAGE VANS 1937/38/47

CFD No.	WORKS No.	DELIVERY	NOTES AND DISPOSAL
10	?/1937	AUG 1952 (Ex CHARENTES)	To CORSICA 1970
20	?/1938	AUG 1952 (Ex CHARENTES)	To CFV 1969.
30	?/1947	FEB 1954 (Ex CHARENTES)	To CFR 1970. VFV 1992.

CFD 4 WHEEL LUGGAGE VAN 1947

CFD No.	WORKS No.	DELIVERY	NOTES AND DISPOSAL
40	?/1947	JULY 1947	To CFR 1970. VFV 1992.

CFD DIESEL LOCOMOTIVES
PETOLAT LOCOTRACTOR 1930

CFD No.	WORKS No.	DELIVERY	DISPOSAL
PE-5	?	JULY 1954 (Ex S&L)	To CFV 1969

CFD 0-6-0 1946/48

CFD No.	WORKS No.	DELIVERY	NOTES & DISPOSAL
X	107A	JUNE 1949	REBUILT FROM Ex CFD YONNE 0-6-2T No.23. BUILT St. LÉONARD No. 726/1897. TO CFV 1969
Y	107B	JUNE 1949	REBUILT FROM Ex CFD YONNE 0-6-2T No.24. BUILT St. LÉONARD No. 727/1897. TO CFV 1969
13	? (1946)	DEC 1960 (Ex S&M)	REBUILT FROM Ex S&M 0-6-0T No.6. BUILT COUILLET No. 695/1883. WITH DRAWN 1968.

CFD MONTMIRAIL BoBo (0-4-4-0) 1963

CFD No.	WORKS No.	DELIVERY	DISPOSAL
040-003	921	OCT 1963	To PROVENCE 1969

CHAPTER SIX

ROLLING STOCK

Carriages

When the first isolated sections of the *Vivarais* were opened in 1890 and 1891, twenty-three bogie carriages built by La Buire were supplied. These comprised twelve Third Class, Nos 4-15, and eleven Composites, Nos 18-28. Of conventional bow-sided design, the Third Class coaches had seven compartments and the Composites six compartments, each with a total capacity of forty passengers. The Composites were divided into six First Class seats, seven Second Class and twenty-seven Third Class, which resulted in at least two compartments of peculiar design! As built, they were fairly basic carriages with only the First Class compartments offering any degree of comfort, the Third Class passengers having to endure wooden slatted seats. In 1925 dynamos were added, enabling electric lighting to be fitted to these, by then, well-used vehicles.

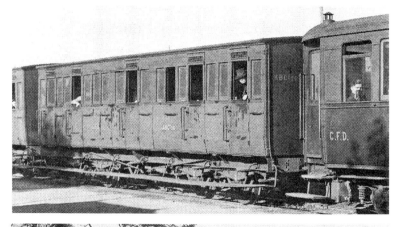

6.1.   La Buire Composite Bogie Coach No.26 was one of the original coaches supplied when the CFD Vivarais opened in 1890. It is seen here at Dunières in 1946 coupled to one of the later Lorraine Dietrich carriages.
(Coll. Dr. Brenot/BVA).

6.2.   De Dietrich Inspection Saloon No.1005 was photographed at Tournon in December 1998. It had once been used by senior officials on prolonged tours and hence the seats could be converted to beds: FAUTEUILS - LITS.
(V.Mitchell)

69

6.3. De Dietrich Composite four wheeled coach ("Henhouse") of 1904, No. 1752, is seen at Le Cheylard in 1952. Note the guards compartment with "birdcage" on the roof. (W. Boegli/BVA).

With the rapid extensions to the system after the turn of the century, additional rolling stock was urgently required. In 1902 De Dietrich constructed a further eleven bogie carriages similar to the La Buire examples of a decade earlier. These comprised three Composites, Nos 1349-1351, and eight Third Class, Nos 1425-1432. At the same time De Dietrich produced a very palatial Directors Saloon, No 1005, in which the CFD hierarchy and their guests could inspect the route in luxury. This four-wheeled carriage replaced a similar vehicle which had originally been used on the *Sein et Marne* before being transferred to other railways in the CFD empire. The De Dietrich Saloon had end balconies while the interior had an open saloon and a well-appointed compartment, which were separated by a toilet and small dining area.

Two years later De Dietrich supplied a further four coaches which, like the Saloon, were four-wheeled vehicles. These comprised two Second/Third Class Composites, Nos 1751/2, and two Third Class, Nos 1801/2. The Composites had four compartments, each with eight seats, two compartments for each class, plus a guards compartment. The Third Class had five compartments, each with eight seats. These small carriages became known as "Henhouses", and with a total of forty passengers in the Third Class versions, it was probably an apt description! The guards compartment in the Composites incorporated a "birdcage" look-out position in the roof, and normally these carriages would be marshalled at the rear of a train.

Following the delivery of the Henhouses in 1904, the passenger stock remained the same until 1927. In that year Lorraine Dietrich, which incorporated the old De Dietrich company, produced some of the most superb carriages ever supplied to a narrow gauge railway. Well known for their luxury motor vehicles, Lorraine Dietrich designed and built these *voitures*, which were far superior to any carriages previously supplied to the CFD. These steel-bodied bogie carriages were produced in two batches. Six Third Class, Nos 1657-1662, were supplied in 1927, while in 1932 a further four completed the complement of passenger carriages. The final four were First and Second Class Composites, Nos 1609-1612. The Third Class vehicles had a capacity of sixty passengers while the later Composites had six First Class seats and forty-four Second Class, plus a toilet. The design was unusual in both versions in that it incorporated a corridor at each end with a compartment alongside, whilst the central section was an open saloon. In 1935 the First/Second Class Composites were modified to become First, Second and Third Class Composites, the First and Second Class seats occupying the two compartments, with the open saloon for the Third Class.

Following the introduction of the railcars during the 1930s, many of the earlier passenger carriages were retired. Some of the chassis were adapted as bogie timber wagons while the bodies often found a new use on the numerous small farms in the area as homes for livestock and poultry. Even some of the later *Grand Voitures* succumbed to the same treatment, with their frames and bogies providing an excellent basis for large capacity timber wagons. Surprisingly, most of the four-wheeled Henhouses outlived the majority of the bogie coaches, which by 1968 had been reduced to a total of five.

Currently preserved are Henhouses Nos 1751, 1801 and 1802, Lorraine Dietrich bogies Nos 1609, 1658, 1659, 1661 and 1662, while the remains of the 1902 De Dietrich bogie No 1427 is in the course of being reconstructed. With the exception of 1659, which is in the VFV stock at Tence, all the preserved *Vivarais* passenger rolling stock is in the care of the CFTM for the CFV operation. Also at Tournon is the splendid De Dietrich Directors Saloon No 1005, which is preserved in immaculate condition.

6.4. Lorraine Dietrich Bogie Composite Coach No. 1609 of 1932 had angled doors and tapered roof ends not unlike the design adopted in 1935 by the GWR for their centenary stock. No. 1609 is seen at Le Cheylard on 24th July 1966. (J. L. Rochaix/BVA).

Luggage vans

In addition to the carriages, a large number of luggage vans, or *Fourgons*, were acquired. Ultimately a total of thirty-two of these four-wheeled vehicles were supplied, although ten of the earlier examples were transferred elsewhere throughout the CFD network between 1905 and 1908. The *Fourgons* also doubled as guards vans and were normally marshalled immediately behind the locomotive on passenger and mixed trains. When used on freight trains they normally occupied the customary rear position of the formation. As with the two Henhouses which incorporated a guards compartment, the *Fourgons* also had a birdcage lookout on the roof. The wooden body incorporated two sliding doors with a diamond window on each side. The guard's compartment was fitted with a stove, the chimney protruding through the roof alongside the birdcage.

The first twelve *Fourgons* were built by La Buire for the initial sections of the system in 1890 and 1891. These comprised two types, six combined luggage and post-vans, Nos 1-6, and six luggage and guards vans, Nos 14-19. It was from these two batches that the ten *Fourgons* Nos 1-4, 6 and 14-18 were distributed throughout the CFD network between 1905 and 1908. Meanwhile, De Dietrich had supplied ten luggage vans, numbered 2045-2054, to a similar design in 1902. These were followed by a further twelve, Nos 2601-2612, two years later. Finally, another two luggage vans, Nos 2626 and 2627, were supplied by De Marly in 1927. From this large collection of *Fourgons* six have survived into preservation. Four are to be found at Tournon for use on the CFV and two at Tence for ultimate use on the VFV.

6.5. Two or the De Dion type NF trucks were recorded at Florac on the CFD Lozère in 1953. These two wheeled vehicles look more like road trailers rather than railway trucks.
(M. Rifault - Coll. J. L. Rochaix/BVA).

6.6. Billard Type RM 1uggage van No.20 was at Le Cheylard on 9th July 1962. Note the bogie protruding beyond the bodywork necessitating the basic sprayguards for the outer pair of wheels.
(J. L. Rochaix/BVA).

6.7. The CFD steel bodied luggage van No.40 was built in 1947. Unlike the Billard wooden bodied vans, this later vehicle was mounted on a four wheeled chassis. (J. L. Rochaix/ BVA).

6.8. De Dietrich luggage van (Fourgon) No. 2607 was built in 1904. Note the diamond shaped windows in the sliding doors. It was photographed at Lamastre on 2nd September 1962. (Photo J. L. Rochaix/BVA).

Freight wagons

A total of 470 wagons of various types was acquired by the CFD for use on the *Réseau du Vivarais*. Of these, fourteen were transferred to other CFD lines, four to *Lozère* in 1904 and ten to *Saône et Loire* in 1912. Fifteen were delivered from the *Lozère* in 1933/4 whilst at the turn of the century fifty-nine wagons had been borrowed from other CFD outposts during the construction of extensions to the *Vivarais*.

These wagons ranged from flat trucks, coal trucks, box vans, cattle trucks and bogie timber wagons. These were supplied from various manufacturers, including La Buire, De Dietrich, Blanc Misseron, Lorraine Dietrich and Decauville between 1890 and 1911, with a further batch from De Marly in 1927.

A total of 126 wagons of various types survive, sixty-six on the CFV and sixty in the care of the VFV. Many of them, particularly those on the CFV, have been restored to their former pristine condition while many others are in a decidedly well-used state of repair.

In addition to the various wagons there was a breakdown crane with a lifting capacity of 4 tonnes. This was a product of De Dietrich and was normally used in company with two flat trucks, fore and aft. With such a small lifting capacity it was suitable for dealing with derailed rolling stock but obviously a derailed locomotive would be beyond its capabilities.

6.9. Van No.19 was converted from one of the original La Buire Fourgons supplied in 1890 and was photographed at Le Cheylard on 9th July 1962. (J. L. Rochaix/BVA).

6.10. The De Dietrich four-tonne crane and its attendant trucks was at Le Cheylard on 9th July 1962. There are conflicting details of the origin of this crane, as it has also been described as being a product of Decauville in 1890. (J. L. Rochaix/BVA).

CFD VIVARAIS PASSENGER COACHES

CFD No.	CONSTRUCTOR	DELIVERY	TYPE	NOTES
4 - 15	LA BUIRE	1890/1	BOGIE 3rd CLASS	
18 - 28	LA BUIRE	1890/1	BOGIE COMPOSITE	
1005	DE DIETRICH	1902	4 WHEEL SALOON	To CFV 1969
1349 - 1351	DE DIETRICH	1902	BOGIE COMPOSITE	
1425 - 1432	DE DIETRICH	1902	BOGIE 3rd CLASS	1427 to CFV 1969
1751 - 1752	DE DIETRICH	1904	4 WHEEL 2nd/3rd CLASS	1751 to CFV 1969
1801 - 1802	DE DIETRICH	1904	4 WHEEL 3rd CLASS	Both to CFV 1969
1657 - 1662	LORRAINE DIETRICH	1927	BOGIE 3rd CLASS	1658/61/62 to CFV 1969 1659 to CFR 1970. VFV 1992
1609 - 1612	LORRAINE DIETRICH	1932	BOGIE 1st/2nd CLASS	1609 to CFV 1969

FOURGONS (LUGGAGE VANS)

CFD No.	CONSTRUCTOR	DELIVERY	TYPE	NOTES
1 - 6	LA BUIRE	1890/1	LUGGAGE/POST	1,4,6 TRANSFERRED to OTHER CFD LINES 1905/08
14 - 19	LA BUIRE	1890/1	LUGGAGE	14-18 TRANSFERRED 1905/08
2045 - 2054	DE DIETRICH	1902	LUGGAGE	
2601 - 2612	DE DIETRICH	1904	LUGGAGE	
2626 - 2627	DE MARLY	1927	LUGGAGE	

CHAPTER SEVEN

PRESERVING THE VIVARAIS

As previously recorded, the CFD retained two Mallets, Nos 403 and 404, in working order during the last decade of the *Réseau du Vivarais'* existence. Officially they were for emergency use but, of course, they were also used on the last remaining steam-hauled passenger workings, such as the Sunday evening trains from St Agrève to Dunières.

7.1.   The FACS special of 5ᵗʰ May 1968 is seen at Intres, double headed by SLM Mallets No. 404 (leading) and No. 403. The success of these final pre-closure special trains provided the impetous for the preservation of at least part or the Vivarais to become a reality. (F. Collardeau).

Aware of the importance of these two surviving locomotives, the CFD, in conjunction with enthusiast organisations such as the *Fédération des Amis des Chemins de Fer Secondaires (FACS)*, arranged numerous "final" steam excursions during the 1960s. Many of these were hauled by 403 proudly wearing its new coat of green paint, often with a water tank mounted on a flat wagon to provide additional water supply. On one momentous occasion, on 5th May 1968, such was the demand for seats on a FACS special from La Voulte to Dunières that both Mallets double-headed the train between Le Cheylard and Dunières with every remaining passenger coach pressed into service. So strong was the feeling of the enthusiasts towards the impending closure that the coaches were daubed with the words *Non a la supression*, while the stations were decked out with bunting and other decorations more akin to an opening than to the final weeks of operation. Ironically, the last steam-hauled train to run successfully under CFD jurisdiction was organised by a British group, the Continental Railway Circle, in September 1968, when 403 worked from Tournon to Dunières. The following week a similar excursion for a German group had to be curtailed as a result of a derailment caused by buffer-locking of the worn coaching stock on the deteriorating track. Consequently steam was absent during the final month of the *Réseau du Vivarais*. This could so easily have been the end of the story, but fortunately some rather determined enthusiasts had other ideas.

Meyzieu

During the 1950s a dedicated group of narrow gauge enthusiasts from the Lyon area held regular meetings and paid many visits to the rapidly diminishing minor lines throughout the country. This group included Jean Arrivetz, Francois Collardeau, Pierre Virot and many other personalities whose names would in due course become associated with the revival of the *Vivarais*. One of their first ventures into preservation was in 1957 when they attempted to save the electrified metre gauge Annemasse-Sixt line in the Haute-Savoie. However, bureaucracy and red tape dictated that the line would close despite the determined efforts of the Lyon-based group. With this experience behind them, they resolved that any future projects would involve railways that they controlled themselves.

With 60cm lines throughout France closing at a rapidly increasing rate, the group scoured the country for locomotives, rolling stock and track, which was transported to a site at Meyzieu on the outskirts of Lyon. Here they constructed a short roadside railway named the *Chemin de Fer Touristique du Meyzieu (CFTM)* which, by 1965, had developed into a profit-making company boasting a stock of seven locomotives and twenty items of rolling stock, mainly drawn from the sugar beet lines in northern France, such as Maizy and Pithiviers. However, the rapid development of the Lyon suburbs meant that Meyzieu would soon be swallowed up and a new home for the railway would have to be found. The Meyzieu line finally closed in 1970 and the rolling stock locked away in some barns on the Rhône islands of Meyzieu. After the Vivarais operation prospered, a new location was sought for the 60cm stock. In 1988 the equipment was moved to a new site at Montalieu, about forty miles east of Lyon. The new line was named the *CFT du Haute-Rhône* and began operations in 1989, the ubiquitous Decauville locomotives hauling some delightful tramcar trailers from Valenciennes and Neuchatel. During the long period of storage some of the equipment was transferred to other 60cm lines that had been developed, many of them on abandoned standard gauge track beds.

In tracing the history of the Meyzieu and Montalieu lines, we have jumped ahead of far more ambitious developments that took place in 1969.

7.2. Couillet 0-6-0T No. 2 from Maizy Sugar Refinery is at work on the CFT Meyzieu with a FACS special on 7th May 1966. (D.Trevor Rowe).

Le Chemin de Fer du Vivarais

During 1968 it was obvious that closure of the *Réseau du Vivarais* was becoming a definite reality. The CFTM group at Meyzieu, having successfully operated their 60cm line since 1960, decided that something of the *Vivarais* should be saved. With only two examples left in working order, one of the 0-6-6-0T Mallets was an obvious choice for preservation, along with some of the remaining passenger coaches. If they were successful in saving these items, a home would have to be found for them. Ideas varied from a short stretch of line to longer, more ambitious, ventures. The suggestions included a short line based at Lamastre, the Doux Gorge section between St Jean de Muzols and

Colombier le Vieux and, most ambitious of all, the whole of the Tournon to Le Cheylard line. Needless to say, the spectacular Le Cheylard to St Agrève line was also discussed, but that was likely to be a very expensive route to operate and maintain, despite being shorter in length than the Tournon line.

Whilst investigating the various possibilities, Jean Arrivetz was at Lamastre in September 1968 examining the track layout and other facilities. By coincidence his visit was on the same day as that of Monsieur Artaud-Macari, the French Inspector General of Land Transport. Seizing the opportunity to discuss the CFTM's various proposals, Jean Arrivetz introduced himself and, by use of some convincing conversation, was invited to join the official party in their railcar for the journey back to Le Cheylard. The outcome was that, after outlining the various proposals, Jean Arrivetz was asked to present a detailed preservation scheme to Artaud-Macari in Paris a week later.

At this period railway preservation was virtually unknown in France and was still developing in Great Britain. However, earlier that year Jean Arrivetz had visited North Wales and was able to produce a large number of photographs of many passengers queuing for tickets at Porthmadog and Tywyn, as well as spending their money in the associated shops. He acknowledges that this, more than anything else, persuaded the General Councils of the Ardèche to give the proposals serious consideration. The proposal to run from Tournon to Le Cheylard was put forward as the first suggestion, the workshops and large engine and carriage sheds at the former headquarters offering many advantages. However, it was agreed that the upper section of the line would be expensive to run and would produce very little extra revenue. Instead the councillors agreed to the line from Tournon to Lamastre being operated as a tourist railway with, hopefully, some freight traffic for extra revenue. Negotiations took place between the CFTM and the other interested parties. These included the councils of the Ardèche, the State as the ultimate owners of the railway, the CFD whose lease was not due to expire until 1985, and the SNCF. Having argued their case to all these official bodies, much valuable assistance being received from the CFD chairman M Francois, the CFTM were granted authority to operate the line from St Jean de Muzols to Lamastre from 15th June 1969. Due to the SNCF not allowing trains to traverse the mixed gauge section, access to Tournon was denied at that time.

7.3. **"Under the wires". SACM Mallet No. 413 departs from Tournon having joined the mixed gauge SNCF track on 29th August 1996. Note the truck immediately behind the locomotive carrying slack coal for Lamastre. (J. F. Organ).**

One major difference between railway preservation in France and in Great Britain is that of possession. Whereas in the latter, preservationists have had to spend vast amounts to purchase their railways and equipment, in France the line still belongs to the State after closure and the prospective new management takes possession of the railway and its equipment without having to pay more than perhaps one symbolic franc.

With the CFTM now subtly renamed *Chemins de Fer Touristiques et de Montagne* [Tourist and Mountain Railway Company], the preserved railway it operated was named *Le Chemin de Fer du Vivarais*. The first train to run under CFTM auspices was in early June, 1969, when railcar 214 ran from Le Cheylard to Lamastre to prolonged applause from the huge crowd upon its arrival. There were also the critics, including some of the former CFD employees, who thought it wouldn't last a month. Happily they were soon to be proved wrong. During the first week of operation, Mallet 404 returned to Le Cheylard and collected goods vans and wagons loaded with much valuable equipment, including hundreds of sleepers. Attached to the rear of the train was De Dion railcar No 207.

**7.4.   Billard A-150-D No. 214 is at Douce Plage with the evening service to Lamastre on 29th August 1996. These railcar services are well patronised by local residents in addition to tourists, especially on market days. Note the modified leading end fitted following the accident in 1970   when 214 and 316 collided at Garnier.
(J .F. Organ)**

The first steam-hauled passenger train under the new regime ran on 22nd June 1969, when 403 hauled four bogie carriages carrying 240 passengers from St Jean de Muzols to Lamastre. Despite the relative inaccessibility of St Jean de Muzols, the CFV ran about two hundred trains and carried over nine thousand passengers, thus convincing the authorities that the operation was a viable proposition. Meanwhile a supporting society was formed, the SGVA [*Sauvegarde et Gestion des Vehicules Anciens* or Association for the Saving and Running of Old Vehicles], which formed working parties to repaint stock, replace rotted sleepers and clear weeds from the track, among many tasks. Despite a comparatively small membership of around three hundred and fifty, the SGVA has raised large sums of money for the railway and provided many hours of free labour.

With a more intensive service envisaged for the following year, it was obvious that four bogie carriages and three henhouses would not be sufficient. In addition, the two surviving Mallets in working order would require heavy overhauls before too long. Consequently, the CFTM directors, along with members of FACS, scoured the remnants of the French metre gauge and some Swiss lines that were in the throes of modernisation schemes. As a result, the stock was considerably enlarged with the arrival of eleven bogie carriages from the *Réseau Breton*, three from the Sarthe Tramway, three from Provence, while Switzerland provided four carriages from the MOB, two from the Brunig and Gruyère, a sole example from Berne-Soleure and three 4-wheeled carriages from Gruyère and Veveysans. FACS also donated a *Réseau Breton Fourgon* to supplement the four *Vivarais* examples already preserved. To provide additional motive power, FACS loaned the CFV their ex-*Réseau Breton* 4-6-0T No E327, which was to remain at the line for ten years before being transferred to the *CF Provence* in 1979.

With so much activity it was obvious that the new venture was a serious proposition, and early in 1970 the SNCF agreed to the CFV having access to Tournon via the mixed gauge track. Although not a cheap option, with an annual fee of over £30,000 for the use of this mile or so of track, the advantages were enormous. Not only was Tournon a far more convenient location for the main terminus of the railway, it also boasted a large engine shed and workshop plus a turntable, water tower and many useful sidings for storage of stock. Having obtained the use of the entire line from Tournon to Lamastre, 403 proudly flying a tricolor hauled a train composed entirely of *Vivarais* origin on 18th April 1970. The rake included a Fourgon, a Henhouse, two Lorraine Dietrich bogie carriages and the unique De Dietrich Inspection Saloon. *Le Mastrou*, the local name for the railway - a derivation of Lamastre, was back with a vengeance. During 1970 nineteen thousand passengers were carried, although the anticipated freight traffic never materialised.

The year 1970 was not without its problems, however. A landslide in the Doux Gorge near Mordane caused many problems, largely because of its inaccessibility, whilst the aforementioned collision between two railcars at Garnier was something which the CFV could have well done without. Despite these setbacks the line continued to prosper and rapidly became the most successful of the preserved lines in France, of which there are now a large number, carrying over sixty thousand passengers annually. When the CFD lease expired in 1985, the CFTM were in a position to take over the ownership of the railway infrastructure and equipment, and the Tournon to Lamastre line really became theirs. This, of course, does not include the section between Tournon and St Jean de Muzols, which is SNCF property.

The CFV is operated by a permanent staff of fifteen, all of whom are very versatile, being able to turn their hands to all manner of tasks required to keep the railway in working order. They are, of course, assisted by volunteers from the SGVA. The whole operation is efficiently controlled by the CFTM from its office in Lyon. Despite the high degree of patronage, the service is not intensive in the way it is commonly found in Great Britain.

A normal day's operation begins when a railcar slips quietly out of Lamastre at 8.00 am, arriving at Tournon an hour later. There is normally one return steam working per day which leaves Tournon at 10.00 am, but at busy periods this is duplicated with a second train which follows about

7.5. Looking almost like a mixed train of CFD days, No. 403 passes under the abutments of the bridge at Douce Plage on 4th September 1996 with a flat truck between the locomotive and fourgon. (J. F. Organ).

fifteen minutes later. The extra trains normally run at weekends or on fête days and other special occasions, their use usually being dictated by the number of advance bookings received. On a normal weekday the railcar is stabled at Tournon during the day, leaving for the hour long return journey to Lamastre at 6.00pm. At weekends and on other special days, the railcar departs for Lamastre at 10.50am and eventually catches up with the steam working, which it follows for the last few miles to the upper terminus. As well as working at a higher speed, the railcar doesn't make a prolonged stop en route at either Colombier-le-Vieux or Boucieu-le-Roi, where the steam working stops for twenty minutes for the locomotive to take water and the passengers to sample the local wine!

Upon arrival at Lamastre at 12.00 noon the locomotive is turned, the fire banked up and the coal bunker topped up with briquettes, after which the crew and passengers alike depart to the town for a long lunch. At weekends and on fête days, should anyone not be able to wait until 4.00pm for the return steam working, the railcar makes an afternoon return trip to Tournon, albeit with an hour-long lunch stop at Colombier-le-Vieux! By 3.00pm the station at Lamastre is getting back to life again, the locomotives take water in readiness for the return journey, leaving at 3.30pm or 4.00pm shortly after the railcar returns. This will make another return trip to Tournon, following the steam service down the valley and returning to its base at Lamastre at 7.15pm. The passengers on the return steam working will be far more subdued following their gourmet lunch breaks. On the outward journey the Doux Gorge would have echoed to the sound of traditional French songs and much joviality from the carriages, particularly at weekends!

7.6.   No.404 is on the turntable at Lamastre on 17ᵗʰ September 1989. This illustration clearly shows the modified cab and bunker fitted shortly after World War II. (J. F. Organ).

Compared with the preserved railways in Great Britain, the commercial aspect of the *Vivarais* in respect of station facilities is very limited. Lamastre has a small sales counter which sells a few books, postcards and a selection of souvenirs. The only bow to commercialisation is the superb Marc Fournier barrel-organ situated in the station booking hall. For a small fee passengers are able to turn the handle and play any tune of their choice from a large repertoire provided by a selection of punched cards. There is also a small display of model railway equipment in the waiting room.

Despite the low-key commercial aspect of the CFV operation, the CFTM is a very sound and efficiently run company. Apart from some initial help from the regional council when they took over the line in 1969, the company has always managed to balance its budget and invariably produces a profit.

7.7. Mallets 404 and 413 prepare to depart from Lamastre with the afternoon trains to Tournon on 17ᵗʰ September 1989. No. 404 will leave first followed by the second train fifteen minutes later. (J. F. Organ).

7.8. SACM Mallet No .413 was recorded at Le Plat with a Lamastre to Tournon train on 1ˢᵗ September 1996. The first coach is one of the former Réseau Breton bogie carriages with their distinctive wooden bodywork. (J. F. Organ).

7.9. No. 403 approaches Douce Plage with the afternoon train bound for Tournon on 3ʳᵈ September 1996. This location, about three miles from Tournon, is one of the most accessible vantage points on the CFV. (Mrs B. Organ).

Locomotives and rolling stock of the CFV

As mentioned in the relevant chapters, most of the surviving CFD equipment was inherited by the CFTM when it took over the Tournon-Lamastre operation in 1969. Initially the locomotive stock consisted of the two surviving SLM Mallets, Nos 403 and 404. Although in working order, they were both due for major overhauls, these being carried out in 1972 and 1973 respectively. As mentioned above, FACS provided the Fives-Lille 4-6-0T No E327 on loan between 1970 and 1979, which was a very useful asset during the early years of the CFV. At the time of closure in 1968 SACM Mallets Nos 413 and 414 were both in store at Le Cheylard, along with the pioneer SLM locomotive No 401. These were all moved to Tournon by road in 1972, 414 being immediately despatched to CFTA de Gray for a complete restoration to working order. This relatively modern locomotive returned to service later the same year, whilst there was a more protracted rebuild for sister engine 413, which eventually returned to service in 1986. No 401 has remained in the sidings at Tournon, having been used as a source of spare parts for its more healthy sisters.

7.10. Nearing journey's end, No. 403 passes the 15th century bridge at Douce Plage bound for Tournon on 3rd September 1996. (J. F. Organ).

7.11. Pinguely 0-6-0T "Bi Cabine" No. 31 from the Tramways Ouest Dauphiné is seen at Tournon in September 1992. This view shows the cab at the smokebox end. By that time, this no longer contained a regulator. (J. F. Organ).

To supplement the locomotives of *Vivarais* origin, machines from elsewhere in France have joined the CFV stock. FACS donated a pair of Corpet 0-8-0Ts dating from 1924, Nos 22 and 24, which came from the Frot Company at Troyes. No 24 was put into working order, spending many years as yard shunter at Tournon until the SNCF finally allowed this former industrial locomotive to traverse the dual gauge track in 1994. No 22 was in poor condition and restoration to working order was not considered to be a viable proposition. Instead it was cosmetically restored and is now to be found on a plinth at the service station on the A7 to the south of Lyon, where it serves as a three-dimensional advertisement for the railway. No.22 has an interesting history having been sent to Jersey in 1943 for use on construction lines for the fortifications. It is probably the only locomotive to have been driven by a German serviceman on British territory! Another locomotive to be found on a plinth advertising the railway is Pinguely 0-6-0T No 103, which is on the riverside esplanade at Tournon. This locomotive arrived in 1971 along with the Twin Cab Pinguely 0-6-0T, No 31, which was donated by FACS. No 31 has been in regular service since its arrival on the lighter mid-week

7.12. Corpet 0-8-OT No. 24 is pictured at Tournon on 29th August 1996. This locomotive is normally used on the lighter mid-week special trains, such as those reserved for school parties. During 1997 it was on loan to the CF Provence during a locomotive crisis for their weekend steam workings. (J. F. Organ).

7.13. Former Réseau Breton Fives-Lille 4-6-0T No. E 327, owned by FACS, was loaned to the CFV between 1970 and 1979. It is now based at Puget-Théniers on the CF Provence where it is seen on 27th March 1983 with a weekend steam working from Nice. (D. Trevor Rowe).

7.14. Blanc-Misseron 0-4-4-0T Mallets Nos 101 and 104 of the PO Corrèze at Tulle in 1959. Both these locomotives are preserved on the two surviving sections of the Vivarais.
(D. Trevor Rowe).

7.15. Pre-season preparations are in progress at Tournon on 23rd March 1997. Former POC Mallet No. 104 is in steam taking water with some of the other locomotives alongside. SACM Mallet No. 413 is nearest the camera. **(F. Collardeau)**

trains and many special workings. Both 31 and Mallet 403 are classified as *Monument Historique*, which hopefully should secure their future!

The only other steam locomotive on the railway is the former *PO Corrèze* 0-4-4-0T Mallet No 104. This Blanc-Misseron machine, dating from 1906, was purchased for an American museum in 1971. It was stored at Tournon pending shipment to the USA but the museum closed before transport could be arranged. Consequently the Mallet remained at Tournon and ultimately was put on static display at Lamastre between 1990 and 1995. Eventually it was returned to Tournon and restored to working order, returning to service in September 1996. During its period on static display it had been painted red in common with the other locomotives on plinths. During its restoration it was repainted in its original POC dark green livery. Officially 104 is too heavy for the *Vivarais* track but the SNCF track bureau of Paris-La Chapelle did some calculations concerning weight per axle and weight of the rail. The locomotive was accepted for use provided the speed did not exceed 30kph or if the tanks were half full, which would allow 35kph. The other option would have been to construct and fit a tender which, apart from the expense, would have precluded the use of the turntables at Tournon and Lamastre. No. 104 is on long term loan from its American owner.

The CFV locomotives sport a variety of liveries in direct contrast to the plain black of the CFD. No 403 has retained the green livery in which it was repainted during the final years of the CFD control of the railway, while 404 was repainted soon after the CFTM takeover in a very attractive maroon with yellow lining, similar to the Midland Railway colour scheme. Following its restoration 414 appeared with a brown livery not unlike that of the London, Brighton and South Coast Railway, and 413 entered service painted a brighter shade of red than that of 404. Nos 31 and 24 are both green, similar to 403.

In addition to the remaining steam locomotives, the CFTM also inherited the two diesel tractors known as X and Y. These useful machines have proved to be invaluable for shunting duties at both Tournon and Lamastre and have also been pressed into service on the occasional passenger train. The small Petolat tractor, No PE-5, also joined the CFV stock in 1969, its Daimler petrol engine being replaced by a small Willème diesel unit in 1983.

Four Billard railcars, Nos 213, 214, 314 and 316 plus three trailers 3, 11 and 22, were also retained for use on the CFV, 314 being repatriated from the CFD *Lozère* where it had been in service since 1967. All have seen regular use on the CFV although 316 has been adapted for use by the PW department. As mentioned above, De Dion railcar No 207 was rescued from store at Le Cheylard in 1969 but has remained at Lamastre since that time awaiting restoration to working order.

Apart from the railcars of CFD origin, a Brissonneau et Lotz articulated "autorail" was acquired from Spain in 1983. This unit was built in 1938 for use on the Toulon-St Tropez-St Raphaël section of the *CF Provence* but since 1948 had been working in Spain between Bilbao and Santander. The power car of this unit is currently at CFTA de Gray undergoing a full mechanical rebuild whilst the trailer car is in store at Tournon.

In 1969 only five Lorraine-Dietrich bogie carriages from the 1927 and 1932 batches and three of the 1904 Henhouses had survived. Four of the bogie vehicles, Nos 1609, 1658, 1661 and 1662, were acquired by the CFTM, along with the three Henhouses 1751, 1801 and 1802. To supplement this limited stock of passenger vehicles the aforementioned carriages from elsewhere in France and Switzerland were acquired during the early years of the CFTM operation. In addition, the De Dietrich Inspection Saloon No 1005 has been retained and sees regular use on special trains. There has been a continual restoration programme with respect to the passenger stock, the majority of which is now in superb condition. The normal daily operation sees a rake of coaches made up mainly of a mixture of Swiss and Breton stock, their open saloon design with end balconies being ideal for use on a tourist railway. The *Vivarais* and *Provence* stock is normally kept in reserve and can usually be seen in use on the weekend "extra" trains when two, and occasionally three, rakes of coaches are required. As in the case of locomotives 403 and 31, many of the carriages are classified as *Monument Historique*, which should safeguard their future survival. Those classified as such include all the *Vivarais* stock, the *Provence* and *Sarthe* bogies and four of the *Breton* vehicles.

Other projects

Since its formation the CFTM has become a very well-respected organisation and this high regard has enabled it to become involved in other projects in addition to its two railways. In 1970 the CFTM was invited to take over the operation of the St Hilaire du Touvet funicular, near Grenoble. This funicular, one of the steepest in the world with an average gradient of 1 in 1.2, was in a very poor state of repair when the CFTM took over in 1970. Following a complete overhaul of the line and its equipment, the funicular was re-opened in 1973 and almost immediately the number of passengers doubled compared with previous operations. By 1977 the St Hilaire funicular was financially viable and was handed back to the local authority's control in excellent condition.

For a number of years Jean Arrivetz and his colleagues at the CFTM have gathered together a collection of trams and buses from around France and Switzerland. These have been stored in a barn at Lamastre pending a decision upon their future. The original intention was a transport museum at Lamastre, but this was abandoned in favour of a project to build a tramline in Lyon at Fourtiere to serve the Roman theatre. Due to a lack of finance because Lyon was at that time also building an underground railway system, this project never materialised. Another suggestion in the early 1990s was to electrify the *Vivarais* track between Tence and Le Chambon and operate the trams along that line in conjunction with the VFV service between Dunières and Tence. Due to a lack of support from the local communities, who now own that part of the *Vivarais* track, this project was also aborted. Another proposal from Lyon to build a 2km tramway between a new park and one of the underground stations has far better possibilities. With support from the Lyon authorities, this new line could well be under way in the near future, whilst other possibilities in Ardèche and elsewhere are also being considered.

The future of the CFV

After more than 30 years running a successful company, the directors of the CFTM are all now in advancing years and beginning to feel the strain of their responsibilities. Negotiations have been taking place during 1997 with the General Council of Ardèche with a view to taking over the infrastructure of the railway and investing much needed capital. Quite possibly financial help could be made available from the Region Rhône-Alps and maybe European funds. For instance the now well worn track will require replacing within the next 10 years.

Obviously the Council would not be in a position to operate the railway. However, at least three large railway companies have expressed an interest in taking over the operation of the Vivarais. The CFTM have meanwhile set out certain conditions:-

Not to stop or restrict the present operation

Not to reduce the number, nor the wages, of the present permanent staff.

Continue to co-operate with SGVA for volunteer assistance in operation and marketing.

All these conditions have been agreed by both the Council and the interested companies. A formal agreement was signed on 24th August 1998 between the CFTM and the Council authorities. This agreement envisages a close working relationship between the two parties. The Council recognises the value of the railway in attracting tourists to the Ardeche which, surprisingly, is the only Department in France without a main line station. The CFTM is anticipating financial support in order to carry out its major infrastructure renewals and equipment overhauls. Also party to the agreement was the French Minister of Transport, who, it is hoped, will be able to bring pressure to bear on the SNCF to reduce its onerous charges for the use of the mixed gauge section of track at Tournon. These currently amount to 10% of the annual turnover.

PRESERVED LOCOMOTIVES AND RAILCARS

LE CHEMIN DE FER DU VIVARAIS (CFV)

No.	TYPE	CONSTRUCTOR	ORIGIN	NOTES
401	0-6-6-0T	SLM	CFD-VIVARAIS	IN STORE AT TOURNON TO BE RESTORED
403	0-6-6-0T	SLM	CFD-VIVARAIS	CLASSIFIED "MONUMENT HISTORIQUE"
404	0-6-6-0T	SLM	CFD-VIVARAIS	
413	0-6-6-0T	SACM	CFD-VIVARAIS	NAMED "MARC SEGUIN"
414	0-6-6-0T	SACM	CFD-VIVARAIS	
104	0-4-4-0T	BLANC-MISSERON	PO CORRÈZE	PRIVATELY OWNED
31	0-6-0T	PINGUELY	QUEST-DAUPHINÉ	TWIN CAB LOCOMOTIVE CLASSIFIED "MONUMENT HISTORIQUE"
103	0-6-0T	PINGUELY	MORBIHAN	ON STATIC DISPLAY AT TOURNON (ESPLANADE)
22	0-8-0T	CORPET	FROT-TROYES	ON STATIC DISPLAY AT A7 SERVICE AREA NEAR LYON
24	0-8-0T	CORPET	FROT-TROYES	
E327	4-6-0T	FIVES-LILLE	RÉSEAU-BRETON	OWNED BY FACS. TRANSFERRED TO PROVENCE 1979.
X	0-6-0 T DIESEL	CFD	CFD-VIVARAIS	REBUILT FROM St. LÉONARD 0-6-2T No. 726
Y	0-6-0T DIESEL	CFD	CFD-VIVARAIS	REBUILT FROM St. LÉONARD 0-6-2T No. 727
PE-5	0-4-0 DIESEL	PETOLAT	SAONE AND LOIRE AND CFD-VIVARAIS	ORIGINALLY FITTED WITH PETROL ENGINE. DIESEL UNIT FITTED 1983.
207	ND	DE-DION BOUTON	CFD-VIVARAIS	IN STORE AT LAMASTRE
213	A-150-D	BILLARD	CFD-VIVARAIS	
214	A-150-D	BILLARD	CFD-VIVARAIS	MODIFIED LEADING END WITH LOWER RADIATOR AND DEEPER WINDSCREEN – 1970/71
314	A-80-D	BILLARD	CFD-CHARENTES AND VIVARAIS	FROM CFD-LOZÈRE 1970
316	A-80-D	BILLARD	CFD-CHARENTES AND VIVARAIS	ADAPTED FOR USE BY CFV PERMANENT WAY DEPARTMENT
ZM-8 + ZR-4		BRISSONEAU ET LOTZ	CF PROVENCE AND BILBAO-SANTANDER (SPAIN)	UNDER RESTORATION

CHAPTER EIGHT

PRESERVATION IN THE HAUTE-LOIRE

Unlike the continued success of the CFV operation between Tournon and Lamastre, the preservation schemes on the northern part of the *Vivarais* between Dunières and St Agrève have been beset with problems. In 1970 an organisation known as *Les Chemins de Fer Régioneaux* [CFR] was granted a concession to operate trains over the route until the CFD lease expired in 1985. The 23-mile route was at the time of its inception the longest tourist railway in Europe, although many trains only operated between Dunières and Tence. Despite being situated in a delightful area of countryside, the line lacks the scenic grandeur of the Tournon-Lamastre line, while none of the towns served by the CFR offered the gastronomic attractions such as those offered at Lamastre. Food is an important consideration to the French tourist! Another important factor was that of accessibility. Whereas Tournon is near the main routes south of Lyon, neither Dunières, Tence or St Agrève have a similar advantage.

8.1. Henschel 0-6-0T No. 99.5611 is at Tence during the CFR operation of the Dunières - St. Agrève line between 1976-86. The locomotive was built in 1903 for the Salzwedel (East Germany) and is currently in private store in Valence.
(Editions Cellard).

8.2. This scene of desolation at St. Agrève was recorded in September 1992. The tracks were still in place but hardly visible under the grass and gravel.
(J. F. Organ).

The CFR continued to operate a limited service until 1987, by which time the lease of the line had been transferred to the various communities along the route of the railway. By this time the permanent way was in need of much attention, for which no money was available, whilst likewise much of the equipment was out of use awaiting attention. After closure in 1987 the track rapidly disappeared beneath the undergrowth while much of the equipment, including all but one of the locomotives, was moved away to Valence for storage. The majority of the once extensive sidings at Dunières vanished under a new road scheme and many of the level crossings between St Agrève and Tence were also "lost" due to road improvements.

In 1992 the local authorities, in a desire to encourage more tourism to the area, allowed another organisation the opportunity to operate the line. The new association, named *Voies Ferrées du Velay* [VFV], began to clear the track between Dunières Ville and Tence and initially ran a few trains from Dunières to Montfaucon during the summer of 1993. By 1994 the line had been re-opened to Tence and a diesel-hauled service operated at weekends and on Wednesdays between June and September.

8.3. Derelict stock stands at Dunières in September 1992. Note the newly laid road over what used to be the metre gauge sidings. (J. F. Organ).

8.4. Former CFD Lozère Diesel Tractor No. 62 waits at Tence with two Swiss coaches on the Voies Ferrées du Velay (VFV) on 28th August 1996. (J. F. Organ).

The CFTM were invited to assist with the operation of the line in conjunction with the VFV in 1995. However, the communities of St Agrève, Le Chambon, Raucoules and Montfaucon left the syndicate, being unable to continue to support the railway due to the financial constraints involved. With the loss of this support and the potential lucrative business from the upper part of the route, the CFTM wisely saw no future in persevering with the venture, whilst the VFV have valiantly continued to offer their limited service to Tence. An attempt to clear the trackbed between Tence and Le Chambon was begun in 1996, but the challenge is enormous. Although the track was still in place, the possibility of trains running to St Agrève in the foreseeable future was remote. Meanwhile progress was made at Dunières during 1996 when the track through the tunnel between Ville and the original northern terminal was relaid. This work was completed at the end of the operating season and the first train since 1987 arrived at Dunières PLM on 6th November 1996. This appropriately comprised a vehicle of *Vivarais* origin, the recently overhauled Billard A 150-D-2, No 222.

8.5.   Former Lozère Diesels Nos 70 and 62 prepare to depart from Dunières Ville with a VFV train for Tence in August 1996. (J. F. Organ).

Locomotives and rolling stock of the CFR and VFV

When the CFR began operating in 1970, its only steam locomotive was the ex-PO *Corrèze* 0-4-4-0T Mallet No 101. This historic Blanc-Misseron machine dating from 1906 was the last narrow gauge steam locomotive to work on a French state-owned line, when the POC closed in 1969. Owned by FACS, it was placed in the care of the CFR on a long term loan, a very generous gesture by its owners. Unfortunately, No 101 was in dire need of a major overhaul and had to be withdrawn from service in 1972. Since that date it remained in the engine shed at Tence until 1994, when members of the VFV began to dismantle it in readiness for a much needed and long overdue rebuild.

In 1971 one of the splendid Piguet 0-6-6-0T Mallets from the *Réseau Breton* arrived at Dunières. Number E417, the last of these impressive engines, built in 1914, never ran on the CFR, being too heavy for the *Vivarais* track. It remained in store at Raucoules until 1995 when it was removed to

Valence and, hopefully, a new life elsewhere. Following the demise of 101, the CFR acquired a pair of small locomotives from the former East Germany. These were a Henschel 0-6-0T dating from 1903 and a Borsig 0-4-0T of 1925 vintage. The Henschel took over all the infrequent steam workings between 1973 and 1987, most of the services being handled by railcars.

A number of railcars were acquired by the CFR, although many were in a very poor condition and only useable as a source of spare parts for the better examples. Most of the services were handled by the only surviving A150-D-2 articulated unit No 222 and A80-D Billard No 313. These were joined by a Billard A150-D-1 No X153 from the *PO Corrèze*, while De Dion No 204 also made an occasional foray along the line. Two of the CFD diesel tractors constructed from redundant steam locomotives, Nos 62 and 70, were obtained from the CFD *Lozère* and used on occasional passenger trains as well as providing banking assistance for the steam-hauled trains up the steep climb from Dunières to Montfaucon.

Apart from Lorraine Dietrich bogie No 1659, all the passenger coaches were obtained from sources other than the *Vivarais*. Four bogie coaches from the *Réseau Breton* were joined by four from Switzerland, including two from the *Rhätische Bahn* [RhB]. The Billard and De Dion railcars and their various trailers were joined by a 1950 Decauville DXW No X232 from the *Réseau Breton*. As with much of the equipment obtained for use by the CFR, this fairly modern machine never ran on the line and remained in store at Tence after closure.

When the VFV began to save the line from extinction in 1993, the only items of equipment available were the two ex-*Lozère* diesel tractors, two Swiss bogie coaches and an open coach converted from a goods wagon. The articulated Billard railcar No 222 was overhauled at Raucoules during 1996, following many years in store at St Agrève, with the intention of it returning to service in 1997. Billard 313 and De Dion 204 were also prepared for a return to service as soon as time and money allow the work to be completed. As mentioned above, the FACS-owned ex-POC Mallet No 101 is the only steam locomotive remaining on the line.

8.6.   Billard A-l50-D-2 Articulated Railcar No. 222 was undergoing restoration to working order at Raucoules-Brossettes on 28th August 1996. (J. F. Organ).

8.7. Another view of No. 222 shows the trailing end car with its blanked off radiator aperture. This machine re-entered service on the VFV in November 1996. (J. F. Organ).

PRESERVED LOCOMOTIVES AND RAILCARS

VOIES FERRÉES DU VELAY (VFV)

No.	TYPE	CONSTRUCTOR	ORIGIN	NOTES
101	0-4-4-0T	BLANC-MISSERON	PO CORRÈZE	UNDER RESTORATION AT TENCE
62	0-6-0 DIESEL	CFD	CFD-LOZÈRE	REBUILT FROM CAIL 2-6-0T (Ex CHARENTES)
70	0-6-0 DIESEL	CFD	CFD-LOZÈRE	AS ABOVE
222	A-150-D-2	BILLARD	CFD-VIVARAIS	
313	A-80-D	BILLARD	CFD-CHARENTES AND VIVARAIS	UNDER RESTORATION
315	A-80-D	BILLARD	CFD-CHARENTES AND VIVARAIS	IN STORE AT TENCE
201	ND	DE-DION-BOUTON	CFD-LOZÈRE	IN STORE (RAUCOULES)
202	ND	DE-DION-BOUTON	CFD-LOZÈRE	IN STORE (RAUCOULES)
204	ND	DE-DION-BOUTON	CFD-VIVARAIS	UNDER RESTORATION
206	ND	DE-DION-BOUTON	CFD-VIVARAIS	IN STORE AT TENCE
X-153	A-150-D-1	BILLARD	ILLE & VILAINE AND PO CORRÈZE	UNDER RESTORATION AT RAUCOULES
52	0-6-0 DIESEL	CFD	CF-PROVENCE	IN STORE AT RAUCOULES

CONCLUSION

In 1968 one of the finest narrow gauge systems closed, along with many other similar railways throughout France. In much the same manner as the infamous Beeching Plan had decimated the railways of Great Britain, the *Vivarais, Breton, Lozère* and *Corrèze* lines all ceased to operate within months of each other, and it appeared as though it was the end of an era.

Fortunately, thanks to the efforts of the CFTM and the VFV, two sections of the *Vivarais* have survived, providing working reminders of this once traditional part of French railway practice. The CFTM in particular, with their highly successful CFV operation between Tournon and Lamastre, have reached the "top league" of preserved railways in Europe. This was vindicated in 1991 when a twinning arrangement was agreed between the CFV and the Ffestiniog Railway, with CFTM President Jean Arrivetz being appointed a Patron of the Ffestiniog. Thus the premier preserved narrow gauge railways of France and Great Britain were justifiably linked.

Although operated on a sound commercial basis, tradition still survives in today's services, with the weekday railcars providing transport for the residents of the Doux Valley to the markets at Tournon and Lamastre. Even though it is unlikely that a calf will be seen being unloaded from a Billard's luggage compartment, together with the local gendarme's new bicycle - whilst the guard sells mushrooms at each station to supplement his wages - some aspects have not changed. It is still not unknown for live poultry and other produce to be found sharing the railcars with the passengers, while the lengthy stops at either Boucieu-le-Roi or Colombier-le-Vieux, which enable today's tourists to have an opportunity to sample the local wine, cheese and other products, have become traditions of more recent years.

One other link with the past that still continues is "whistling for the Countess". Shortly after leaving Boucieu-le-Roi the drivers of the steam locomotives sound their shrill whistles when passing the Château de Chazotte, the former home of the Countess of Chazotte. This venerable lady was a great supporter of the railway, and when it closed in 1968 she kept the shutters of the château firmly shut. When the first trains ran under the new regime they were opened again to the accompaniment of a whistle from the locomotive. Although the Countess died in 1982, the tradition is still continued.

The CFV is now firmly established and will continue to maintain the best traditions of the line. It has become more accessible to British visitors with the advent of Eurostar and TGV services. Travellers from London can reach Valence in about six hours, with one change at Lille. A 10 minute northward journey to Tain-L'Hermitage-Tournon station is followed by a 20 minute walk to reach the west bank of the Rhone by means of a suspension bridge. The nearest accommodation is Hotel Azalees in Avenue du Gare, Tournon. (Tel. 0033 475 080 523) and Ffestiniog Travel offers a reliable rail ticket booking service (Tel. 01766 512340). The twinning of Europe's premier narrow gauge steam railways was a far sighted act of long term benefit to both spectacular lines.

VIVE LE VIVARAIS

BIBLIOGRAPHY

Although much has been written about the Reseau du Vivarais in many books and magazine in the past, only the book written by Jean Arrivetz and Pascal Bejui specifically covers the history of the Vivarais in detail. This must he regarded as the definitive album on the subject.

Books

LES CHEMINS DE FER DU VIVARAIS by Jean Arrivetz and Pascal Bejui.
Presses et Editions Ferroviaires 1986 and 1991.

LA FRANCE A VOIE ETROITE by Marc Dahlstrom.
Collection Rail-Amateur 1989.

NARROW GAUGE RAILWAYS OF EUROPE by Peter Allen and P.B. Whitehouse,
Ian Allan 1959 and 1961.

ON THE NARROW GAUGE by P.B. Whitehouse.
Thomas Nelson and Sons 1964,

FRENCH MINOR RAILWAYS by W.J.K. Davies,
David and Charles / Macdonald 1965

THE END OF THE LINE by Bryan Morgan.
Cleaver-Hume 1955.

THE TOURIST RAILWAYS OF FRANCE by Richard Haworth.
Rapid Transit Publications 1995.

Magazine Articles

LE CHEMIN DE FER DU VIVARAIS by Jean Arrivetz.
Chemins de fer Regionaux et Urbains No. 237 1993,

LE RESEAU DU VIVARAIS DES CHEMINS DE FER DEPARTEMENTAUX by M,
Jean-Claude Riffaud
Magazine des Tramways a Vapeur et des Secondaires No 13 1980/81

THE RESEAU DU VIVARAIS by John Snell
Trains Illustrated (Ian Allan) 1970,

RESEAU DU VIVARAIS 1967 By Roger Capewell. The Narrow Gauge No. 53. March 1970
CF du VIVARAIS - "The greatest of the little trains of France" by Mike Atherton Railway
World (Ian Allan) August 1990

VAPEUR ON VIVARAIS by Richard Harrison, The Narrow Gauge No 133 Winter 1991/2.

THE TOURIST RAILWAYS OF FRANCE by Jean Arrivetz and Michel Braun Railway World
(Ian Allan) June 1995

EUROPEAN STEAM SCENE, FRANCE. CFV by John Organ RAILWAY WORLD (Ian Allan)
March 1998

INDEX TO PLACE NAMES
CHAPTERS 1, 2, 3, 7 & 8
(Page Nos. in italics refer to pictures and diagrams)

MP Middleton Press

Easebourne Lane, Midhurst, West Sussex. GU29 9AZ Tel: 01730 813169 Fax: 01730 812601
If books are not available from your local transport stockist, order direct with cheque, Visa or Mastercard, post free UK.

BRANCH LINES
Branch Line to Allhallows
Branch Lines around Ascot
Branch Line to Ashburton
Branch Lines around Bodmin
Branch Line to Bude
Branch Lines around Canterbury
Branch Lines around Chard & Yeovil
Branch Line to Cheddar
Branch Lines around Cromer
Branch Lines to East Grinstead
Branch Lines to Effingham Junction
Branch Lines around Exmouth
Branch Line to Fairford
Branch Line to Hawkhurst
Branch Line to Hayling
Branch Lines to Horsham
Branch Line to Ilfracombe
Branch Line to Kingswear
Branch Lines to Launceston & Princetown
Branch Lines to Longmoor
Branch Line to Looe
Branch Line to Lyme Regis
Branch Lines around March
Branch Lines around Midhurst
Branch Line to Minehead
Branch Line to Moretonhampstead
Branch Lines to Newport (IOW)
Branch Line to Padstow
Branch Lines around Plymouth
Branch Line to Selsey
Branch Lines around Sheerness
Branch Line to Tenterden
Branch Lines to Torrington
Branch Lines to Tunbridge Wells
Branch Line to Upwell
Branch Lines around Weymouth
Branch Lines around Wimborne
Branch Lines around Wisbech

NARROW GAUGE BRANCH LINES
Branch Line to Lynton
Branch Lines around Portmadoc 1923-46
Branch Lines around Porthmadog 1954-94
Two-Foot Gauge Survivors

SOUTH COAST RAILWAYS
Ashford to Dover
Brighton to Eastbourne
Chichester to Portsmouth
Dover to Ramsgate
Hastings to Ashford
Portsmouth to Southampton
Southampton to Bournemouth
Worthing to Chichester

SOUTHERN MAIN LINES
Bromley South to Rochester
Charing Cross to Orpington
Crawley to Littlehampton
Dartford to Sittingbourne
East Croydon to Three Bridges
Epsom to Horsham
Exeter to Barnstaple
Exeter to Tavistock
Faversham to Dover
Haywards Heath to Seaford
London Bridge to East Croydon
Orpington to Tonbridge
Salisbury to Yeovil

Swanley to Ashford
Tavistock to Plymouth
Victoria to East Croydon
Waterloo to Windsor
Waterloo to Woking
Woking to Portsmouth
Woking to Southampton
Yeovil to Exeter

EASTERN MAIN LINES
Fenchurch Street to Barking

COUNTRY RAILWAY ROUTES
Andover to Southampton
Bournemouth to Evercreech Jn.
Burnham to Evercreech Junction
Croydon to East Grinstead
Didcot to Winchester
Fareham to Salisbury
Frome to Bristol
Guildford to Redhill
Porthmadog to Blaenau
Reading to Basingstoke
Reading to Guildford
Redhill to Ashford
Salisbury to Westbury
Stratford Upon Avon to Cheltenham
Strood to Paddock Wood
Taunton to Barnstaple
Wenford Bridge to Fowey
Westbury to Bath
Woking to Alton
Yeovil to Dorchester

GREAT RAILWAY ERAS
Ashford from Steam to Eurostar
Clapham Junction 50 years of change
Festiniog in the Fifties
Festiniog in the Sixties
Isle of Wight Lines 50 years of change
Railways to Victory 1944-46

LONDON SUBURBAN RAILWAYS
Caterham and Tattenham Corner
Charing Cross to Dartford
Clapham Jn. to Beckenham Jn.
Crystal Palace and Catford Loop
East London Line
Finsbury Park to Alexandra Palace
Holborn Viaduct to Lewisham
Kingston and Hounslow Loops
Lewisham to Dartford
Lines around Wimbledon
London Bridge to Addiscombe
North London Line
South London Line
West Croydon to Epsom
West London Line
Willesden Junction to Richmond
Wimbledon to Epsom

STEAMING THROUGH
Steaming through Cornwall
Steaming through the Isle of Wight
Steaming through Kent
Steaming through West Hants
Steaming through West Sussex

TRAMWAY CLASSICS
Aldgate & Stepney Tramways
Barnet & Finchley Tramways

Bath Tramways
Bournemouth & Poole Tramways
Brighton's Tramways
Camberwell & W.Norwood Tramways
Clapham & Streatham Tramways
Dover's Tramways
East Ham & West Ham Tramways
Edgware and Willesden Tramways
Eltham & Woolwich Tramways
Embankment & Waterloo Tramways
Enfield & Wood Green Tramways
Exeter & Taunton Tramways
Gosport & Horndean Tramways
Greenwich & Dartford Tramways
Hampstead & Highgate Tramways
Hastings Tramways
Holborn & Finsbury Tramways
Ilford & Barking Tramways
Kingston & Wimbledon Tramways
Lewisham & Catford Tramways
Liverpool Tramways 1. Eastern Routes
Liverpool Tramways 2. Southern Routes
Maidstone & Chatham Tramways
North Kent Tramways
Portsmouth's Tramways
Reading Tramways
Seaton & Eastbourne Tramways
Shepherds Bush & Uxbridge Tramways
Southampton Tramways
Southend-on-sea Tramways
Southwark & Deptford Tramways
Stamford Hill Tramways
Thanet's Tramways
Victoria & Lambeth Tramways
Waltham Cross & Edmonton Tramways
Walthamstow & Leyton Tramways
Wandsworth & Battersea Tramways

TROLLEYBUS CLASSICS
Croydon Trolleybuses
Bournemouth Trolleybuses
Hastings Trolleybuses
Maidstone Trolleybuses
Reading Trolleybuses
Woolwich & Dartford Trolleybuses

WATERWAY ALBUMS
Kent and East Sussex Waterways
London to Portsmouth Waterway
Surrey Waterways
West Sussex Waterways

MILITARY BOOKS and VIDEO
Battle over Portsmouth
Battle over Sussex 1940
Blitz over Sussex 1941-42
Bombers over Sussex 1943-45
Bognor at War
Military Defence of West Sussex
Secret Sussex Resistance
Sussex Home Guard
War on the Line
War on the Line VIDEO

OTHER BOOKS and VIDEO
Betwixt Petersfield & Midhurst
Changing Midhurst
Garraway Father & Son
Index to all Stations
South Eastern & Chatham Railways
London Chatham & Dover Railway